THE THEATRE LIBRARY ASSOCIATION BOOK AWARDS

Two awards are presented annually for books of unusual merit and distinction in the fields served by the Association.

The George Freedley Award, *established in 1968, honors work in the field of theatre published in the United States. Only books with subjects related to live performance will be considered. They may be biography, history or criticism.*

The Theatre Library Association Award, *established in 1973, honors a book published in the United States in the field of recorded performance, which includes motion pictures, radio and television.*

Works ineligible for both awards are textbooks; anthologies; collections of essays previously published in other sources; reprints; works on dance, ballet and opera; plays and similar dramatic works. Translations of significant works, other than play texts, will be considered. Entries will be judged on the basis of scholarship, readability and general contribution of knowledge to the fields served by the Association. No galley sheets or proofs will be accepted. Books nominated for awards must be published in the calendar year prior to the presentation of the awards and must be received no later than March 1 of the year following publication.

Nominations are to be submitted in writing to the Chair, Book Awards Committee, in care of the Theatre Library Association, 111 Amsterdam Avenue, New York, NY 10023.

PERFORMING ARTS RESOURCES, *the annual publication of the Theatre Library Association, is designed to gather and disseminate scholarly articles dealing with the location of resource materials relating to theatre, film, television and radio; descriptions, listings, or evaluations of the contents of such collections, whether public or private; and monographs of previously unpublished original source material.*

All manuscripts must be submitted cleanly typed, one side only, double-spaced and adhering to the style and method described in the MLA Style Sheet, Second Edition. *Photographs and illustrations may be used at the discretion of the editors.*

Please submit manuscripts with covering letter and return postage to:

Performing Arts Resources
c/o B.N. Cohen-Stratyner
300 Riverside Drive
New York, New York 10025

PERFORMING ARTS RESOURCES

Edited by Ginnine Cocuzza
and
Barbara Naomi Cohen-Stratyner

VOLUME EIGHT

Published by the Theatre Library Association

Headquarters: 111 Amsterdam Avenue, New York, NY 10023
Membership dues: $20 personal, $25 institutional

The Library of Congress cataloged this serial as follows:

Performing Arts Resources
Vols. for 1974- issued by the Theatre Library Association
ISSN 0360-3814
1. Performing arts–Library resources–United States–Periodicals.
I. Theatre Library Association
Z6935.P46 016.7902'08 75-646287
ISBN 0-932610-04-8

Produced by BookCrafters, Inc., Chelsea, Michigan
Manufactured in the United States of America

TABLE OF CONTENTS

ILLUSTRATIONS

ILLUSTRATIONS

FROM THE EDITORS

We are pleased to add *Stage Design: Papers from the 15th International Congress of SIBMAS* to the *Performing Arts Resources* published by the Theatre Library Association. This valuable compendium presents many of the papers presented at the Fall 1982 conference dedicated to, as its title read, Stage Design: problems of collecting, cataloguing and conserving documents. The congress, held in New York City, brought together scholars, curators, conservationists, archivists and designers in an effort to promote understanding and greater interaction. Papers, workshops, tours, demonstrations and discussions in French and English were provided for the visiting participants from the United States, Europe and Africa.

This volume organizes papers around two sub-themes that emerged during the SIBMAS congress – scenic documents as valuable tools that defy time and as fragile victims to decay. We begin and end the volume with illustrated case studies on the collection and preservation of costume plates in Canada and the United States and on the reconstruction and cataloguing of entire theater buildings in Western Europe. We also include theoretical papers from the United States and both Western and Eastern Europe on the value of scenery models and plates as documents for historians and museum-goers, as well as the difficulties of mere language (or languages) in dealing with the terminology of the visual. Perhaps the most important paper is the first in the volume, a plea from Nigeria's Cecilia Folasade Adedeji for the establishment of an institution for the preservation of African stage design, a request to be allowed to discover the problems of cataloguing and preservation that our own collections attempt to solve.

Performing Arts Resources will continue to make available reference material that will augment library collections and give researchers access to rare material, as well as articles enabling librarians archivists and researchers to locate, identify and classify information on theatre, film, the broadcast media and popular entertainment forms. We will alternate monographs with compendium volumes on single subjects. We welcome our readers' comments and suggestions.

Ginnine Cocuzza
Barbara Naomi Cohen-Stratyner

Stage Design:

Papers from the 15th International Congress of SIBMAS

PREFACE

The International Association of Libraries and Museums of the Performing Arts was founded in 1954 as a section of the International Federation of Library Associations. Since 1976, it has been autonomous, but maintains strong ties to IFLA, ICOM (International Council of Museums), IFTR (International Federation for Theatre Research), and ITI (International Theatre Institute), as well as the American associations: Theatre Library Association and the American Society for Theatre Research. The association is usually referred to by the acronym SIBMAS, derived from the French equivalent of the English name: Societé Internationale des Bibliotheques et Musees des Arts du Spectacle.

SIBMAS has as its stated aims: the promotion of research, practical and theoretical, in the documentation of the performing arts; the establishment of permanent international contacts among specialized libraries, museums and documentation centers; and the coordination of the work and discoveries of members and the facilitation of international exchanges of and among them.

The contributions of the organization to the field of performing arts documentation are embodied in a number of ongoing activities. It organizes a biennial international congress which concentrates on a single theme in the performing arts discipline. Papers are read by librarians, curators and scholars and are later gathered into a publication which goes out to the members and others interested in the subject. The themes of the last congresses have been:

1976-Vienna	"The Media and Sources in the Documentation of Theatre"
1978-Barcelona	"Documentation in the Service of the Cultural Diffusion of the Performing Arts, Especially in South America, Africa, the Middle East and the Far East."
1980-Belgrade	"The Use of Theatrical and Other Records for Artistic and Technical Purposes: Methodology"

SIBMAS has five standing work committees, all of which report to the members at the biennial congress. The first, referred to as SANDAS, oversees the progress of mechanized and computerized library systems. The other committees are the Theatre/Education/Documentation Committee, the Basic Bibliography Committee, the Committee on National Centers and the Committee on Audio-Visual Materials. The activities of the committees, reports on exhibitions, meetings and conferences, as well as other miscellaneous information are published in a bulletin co-sponsored by the International Federation for Theatre Research and prepared in Amsterdam.

SIBMAS has worked actively with Professor André Veinstein of the University of Paris in the updating of the definitive directory, *Performing Arts Libraries and Museums of the World.* Work on the third edition is in progress and there is hope that it will be published in English and French in 1983.

Members of SIBMAS also receive a copy of *L'Information du Spectacle* (out of Paris) and are urged to submit articles to *Theatre Research International* (out of Glasgow).

The importance of the meetings cannot be overestimated. For the first time, it brought enormous amounts of information via human resources to this country and generated interaction among American, European, Oriental and Third World counterparts. It gave an opportunity for Americans who have been unable to attend the overseas congresses a chance to meet with colleagues who share common problems and may offer specific solutions. The end result, it is hoped, was to create a sense of community among Americans and their international colleagues. It is expected that many more Americans will contribute to the congress than they have done in the past.

Since most American performing arts collections have large holdings of scenery and costume designs, the theme of the 15th Congress was especially attractive. All collections share many common problems in collecting, cataloguing and conserving stage designs but these documents remain among the most significant from both historical and artistic aspects. From the Renaissance on, the stage artist has been responsible for creating the milieu for actors. Throughout his history as collaborator in the production of plays, operas, ballets, circuses and spectacles, he has been called upon to enhance, enliven, define and otherwise materialize what the writer, composer, lyricist, director and choreographer have devised. He has done it ultimately, of course, in the three dimensions of the proscenium or other stage mode; his fate has been to see his creation dismantled and destroyed when the production's life has run its course. Since he is aware from the onset that his work only lives in the present, he has accepted the ephemerality of his contribution as a condition of his participation in the larger canvas of stage production.

From the time of such early Renaissance artists as the Bibienas and Serlio, the stage designer may have also been a painter, architect and, sometimes, mechanical engineer. He has worked in pencil, crayon, pen and ink, watercolor, gouache, oil and three-dimensional maquette. In the usual course of events, his sketch in whatever form has enjoyed no longer life than the theatrical occasion for which it was designed. To quote the late Donald Oenslager, one of America's foremost stage artists:

> Few designers are good housekeepers. Most are not preservationists, and so their sketches tend to disappear. They have no sense of allegiance to posterity. Unfortunately for theatre historians, rarely does a theatre drawing boast of the artist's signature or the date or name of the production for which it was designed.

Oenslager went on to say that whenever the designer's sketches survive, they seem "doomed to an afterlife on library shelves or to languish in museum vaults whence they are occasionally exhumed for special exhibitions."

The "afterlife" to which Oenslager alludes almost slightingly has represented both a bane and a blessing for theatre curators and librarians. In a great many cases, long after the scripts have been lost or the actors have vanished, the one testament to a theatrical performance which has managed to surface is the stage design. Often spattered with stage paint or coffee, written over in the special language used by artist and craftsman, frequently coded with cryptic instructions and very often, totally unidentified, it becomes the problem of the curator and librarian to identify, date, clean, conserve and catalogue.

Although many of the designs are examples of supreme draftsmanship and worthy to hang in museums, others are rough drawings and merely intimations of how the stage and actors will ultimately be dressed. Some are painters' elevations, floor plans, pencil sketches for what will become elaborate costumes, or sections of detail of fancy moldings, but all are precious to the curator, librarian and scholar.

In focussing its attention on stage designs, the congress emphasized to the theatrical community the importance of these documents to performing arts collections. Because of restrictive tax laws both here and abroad, stage designs are frequently sold, given to friends or dispersed in other ways, which has been making the collecting of them more and more difficult. In showing genuine concern for their care and conservation, the organization hopes to attract donations of stage designs to established collections.

SIBMAS, either as an independent organization or a branch of IFLA, had never met in the United States. Although many of the members are aware of the richness of American collections in the performing arts, few had ever visited them. They were unacquainted with the extent of America's vast museums and library systems. Because several of this country's most important collections are housed in New York under the auspices of the Museum of the City of New York, The New York Public Library, the Players Club, the Shubert Archive, the Museum of Broadcasting and the Songwriters Hall of Fame, it made sense that New York should be the site of an American congress.

Since the art of the designer has been the subject of ever-increasing research and critical commentary, as well as continual exhibition, the theme of the SIBMAS Congress in 1982 was especially appropriate. It would be impossible to cite all of the recent books and exhibitions on stage design, but several have been noteworthy. The Theatre Collection at the Museum of the City of New York opened its exhibition "Designs to Dazzle: Showgirl Costumes of the Past Fifty Years on Broadway" on October 6, 1981. An exhibition devoted to the designs of Boris Aronson has just closed at the Astor Gallery of the Museum of Performing Arts at Lincoln Center and another, "German Nineteenth Century Stage Designs," from the Munich Theatre Museum, recently ended a two-month stay at the Cooper-Hewitt Museum. Such American designers as Donald Oenslager, Howard Bay and Eldon Elder have written eloquently on stage design in America joining their many European counterparts in the celebration of this art of the theatre.

An invitation was tendered to the members at Belgrade, Yugoslavia, by Dr. Mary C. Henderson, Curator of the Theatre Collection of the Museum of the City of New York and former editor of *Performing Arts Resources,* to convene the 15th SIBMAS Congress in New York under the sponsorship of the Museum of the City of New York and the Library and the Museum of the Performing Arts at Lincoln Center. The suggestion was unanimously accepted.

In May, 1981, the Annual Meeting of the Council of SIBMAS was held at the Museum of Decorative Arts in Copenhagen to discuss the work of the organization and to prepare for the 1982 congress. The Council set the theme of the congress and agreed that the title should be as follows: "Stage Design: Problems of Collecting, Cataloguing and Conserving Documents." Dr. Henderson was appointed Secretary-General of the Congress.

The congress itself took place in New York from August 29 through September 4, 1982. It was made possible through the assistance of a research grant from the National Endowment for the Humanities, with grants in support from the European American Bank, the Friends of the Theatre Collection, Museum of the City of New York, and the Theatre Library Association. As well as panels, discussions and plenary meetings, the attending scholars and designers were treated to lecture-demonstrations and tours of many of New York's theater archives, among them, the Museum's own collections, The New York Public Library's Billy Rose Theatre Collection and Library and Museum of Performing Arts, and the Austrian Institute's exhibit on Austrian theatre, as well as [William] Gillette's Castle, the O'Neill family summer cottage, "Monte Cristo," and the Goodspeed Opera House in nearby Connecticut.

Like the tours, some of the conference's presentations could not be included in this volume. They range from valuable discussions on computerization to a slide show by Dr. Oskar Pausch on "Newly Discovered Frescoes Testifying to Medieval Theatre in Vienna." Previously published papers could also not be reprinted herein.

OPENING REMARKS

by Eva Steinaa

Dear guests, colleagues and friends:

It is with great pleasure, gratitude and emotion that I welcome all participants at this 15th congress of SIBMAS in New York, the first one to be held on another continent, – a new world to many of the European (and African) participants, unfortunately not so numerous as we would have hoped for economical reasons. Your dollar is too expensive! In return we greet with much pleasure the many American participants to whom SIBMAS is a new world. I am convinced that your local knowledge and experience within theatre documentation will be very inspiring to all the SIBMAS members coming from over there.

STAGE DESIGN, the theme of this congress, seems to be a happy choice judging from the number of papers which will be delivered within the next days about this very important part of a theatre production.

We all know that stage designers as well as actors should only be servants to a given text which they must respect. However, we have often had the experience of seeing a classical play find new life because a director together with his stage designer have seen the text with new eyes. A successful performance is the result of a close cooperation. But all the same you feel the artist's personality in everything he creates for the stage.

It is up to us who work in the museums and libraries of the performing arts to try to preserve this art of illusion for the future– to know how to collect, catalogue and conserve the documents of stage design. It is not always so simple as was the case with a performance of our Danish classical playwright Ludvig Holberg which took place in the garden of my museum, the Museum of Decorative Art in Copenhagen, this summer. The setting for the play was a platform, the walls of the museum building and the trees of the garden, and apart from the

---

EVA STEINAA, of the Museum of Decorative Art in Copenhagen, is President of SIBMAS.

costumes, a horse and a hen, the only prop was a small garden bench which is not kept for posterity in *my* little garden.

Looking over the programme you will find that we are going to work seriously and concentratedly with the problems of conserving theatrical documentation. Thanks to the organizing talent of Dr. Mary Henderson we will be able to glimpse at and work in two of the main theatre-institutions in New York.

I was very happy when we got the invitation at the Belgrade congress to come to New York. Last year in Copenhagen we discussed all the problems of economic and practical order concerned with a congress, and I knew that more than any, Mary would be able to carry through the very ambitious plans about this congress. I am looking forward to the days we are going to spend together in the name of SIBMAS under your skilled direction. We would like to thank the generous sponsors, you and your staff beforehand for all the preparations you have made to accommodate us and make us feel at home in this new world.

KEYNOTE ADDRESS

By Howard Bay

The designer is an individual who functions as a firm – through feast and famine. In more hectic periods he or she will employ, temporarily, one or two assistants for drafting and shopping. Conferences, furniture, drapery and upholstery procurements, shop and theatre supervision, office and bookkeeping are all on top of the artwork: renderings, working drawings, painters' elevations, swatches, specifications, and samples. And, of course, there are renovations due to script and directorial changes. What I am insinuating is that the designer hasn't time to worry about posterity. Anyway, our renderings are promises, not the end product. It behooves us to donate sketches to producers, authors and directors when they request same. There was no yardstick for evaluating our little watercolors until a London gallery opened a New York branch exclusively devoted to set and costume designs. Now the tax people grudgingly acknowledge the value of gifts to museums and libraries. P.S., the gallery went out of business.

There is the problem of whether we practice a craft or an art. Both, I believe. The blurring of the distinction between fine and applied art has helped.

The large question is: what is the value of assembling these partial memories of ephemeral dramatic events? It is because the visual arm of stage creation is one of the best reflections of the progress of *popular* art. Often corny, sometimes sloppy and diffused, we always deal with human concerns and surroundings. You can cram your dead storage areas with the Bauhaus, with hard edge, color fields, snapshots of earthworks, minimal and conceptual numbers as there is very little of lasting interest since de Kooning and Steinberg. Laying aside the procurement difficuties, what would constitute a fair survey of modern American design? Automatically, the genuine, original biggies: Urban, Jones, Bel Geddes, Simonson; plus Bernstein, Throckmorton, Sovey,

---

Noted designer HOWARD BAY was responsible for the scenery for many of Broadway's most memorable productions, among them, the successful musicals *Up in Central Park, The Music Man* and ***Man of La Mancha.***

Platt, Bragdon, Harkrider, Gorelik, Stewart Chaney and a couple of talents that have been lost: John Wenger and Herman Rosse. The next batch: Oenslager, Mielziner, Aronson, Harry Horner, du Bois, Albert Johnson, Sharaff, Minnelli, Lemuel Ayres, Peter Larkin, Oliver Smith, George Jenkins . . . Bay. The two in that list that need attention are Albert Johnson and Lemuel Ayres. Albert completely renovated the musical comedy design of the Urban tradition and Lem added an elegance to the genre. More recently we have Robin Wagner, Santo Loquasto, Ming Cho Lee in opera, Rouben Ter-Arutunian in dance, costumers Willa Kim and Pat Ziprodt, as well as designers very busy in regional companies such as John Conklin and David Jenkins. A partial listing to be sure but if you can find samples from a goodly portion you will be doing fine.

When we put together the U.S.A./I.T.I. exhibit not long ago, it took two years, many willing volunteers – and broke the bank at International Theatre Institute. It was the first comprehensive exhibition of American work since 1935. And there were holes in it because much contemporary stuff is only devised in model form and models are fragile and tend to disappear. Generally there is a lopsided view of stage design because only the pictorial examples look pretty and therefore are shown and are reproduced: musicals such as Oliver Smith's *High Button Shoes* and *My Fair Lady,* Lem Ayers' *Bloomer Girl* and my *Music Man* and *Up In Central Park.* Renderings were never made for *A Chorus Line* or *Dreamgirls* or to really go back: *Dead End* or *One Third of a Nation.*

I knocked out the "preliminary" sketch for *Man of La Mancha* four months after its opening because it was for the cover of *Saturday Review.* In the scurry and bustle of mounting a show, the designer gives little thought to polishing artwork that will be a memorial for all time. Robert Edmond Jones made lovely sketches while Edward Gordon Craig did little else – besides the rhetoric, that is. The only constructive thought I can offer aside from the laborious, time consuming and often fruitless chasing of designs for past triumphs, is this: peruse the upcoming theatrical season, select the most exhilarating prospect from a scenic, costume and lighting viewpoint, follow the designers through the production process and in an end exhibit display tentative doodles, roughs, color renderings and/or models, photos of the execution in the assorted shops, final fittings, tech and dress rehearsals – In other words through opening night. The citizens out there are fascinated by backstage doings and how else can one recapture the gestalt, of say, *Dreamgirls* or *Cats?* Such an enterprise should counteract the devotion to the color sketch as the sole artifact in theatrical design. Which leads into the business of the prominence awarded to fine artists who now and then condescend to embellish the stage. Picasso was the exception, as always, because he took the trouble to examine the special requirements of the theatre – as he had adjusted to the needs of sculpture, ceramics and engraving. The same does not apply to other modern giants who occasionally put blownup easel paintings behind performers. The second string, more illustrative artists have fared better behind the footlights: Dufy, Tchelitchev, Rauschenberg and Hockney . . . Bakst, Golovin, Benois, Roerich, Anisfeld, Larionov and Exeter were theatre artists. We commercial types do not refine a single style but labor in all styles – whatever is appropriate for a given dramatic script.

In summation I must repeat the obvious: our gifts to culture only find their expression in the total theatrical event in front of paying customers. The only way our contribution can be partially captured is by the accumulation of records along the way – concrete data of the collaborative *process* of production – a process in which the designers are key elements.

AFRICAN STAGE DESIGN: PROBLEMS OF COLLECTING, CATALOGUING AND CONSERVING DOCUMENTS

By Cecilia Folasade Adedeji

Africa is a continent with many countries; each consisting of a multiplicity of ethnic groups, each with her own traditions and cultures, religion, rituals and festivals from which the theatre could be said to have developed.

Stage design includes both the spatial environment of performance and stage setting. In Africa today, stage design in its elaborate style, the proscenium stage and set construction of the Western and European world is being copied. Whereas in traditional African societies, the concept of stage is just a space for performance. It is created in the open-air as arena stage or theatre in the round. It could be in the market place, at street corners, in the courtyards of Chiefs and Kings, or at shrines and temples where we believe that the gods are present as guests. Thus the environment of theatrical presentation is both spatial and temporal. The acting arena or stage is a place of transformation. The performers are symbolic representations of gods, ancestors and spirits who act to communicate with the people.

There are no specially built playhouses. Since the African is very imaginative, a staged play does not require specifics or elaborate sets. Performances are designed as presentational projections involving the use of the imagination to reflect on the symbolics of stage presentation. Costumes and stage props are equally symbolically presented because the characters are types.

European theatrical excursions into Africa occurred largely during the second half of the nineteenth century. The early performances given were variety entertainments, concerts and comic shows. They were held in public halls, school halls and other spatial structures designed not specifically as theatres. These kinds of entertainment were quickly adopted by the Africans because they came very close to their own traditions of theatrical performances. There was hardly any

---

CECILIA FOLASADE ADEDEJI is the Serials Librarian for the Ibadan University Library in Nigeria.

attempt at the stage design. Wherever it existed it was an adhoc arrangement which lacked permanence.

The contemporary situation has seen the emergence of permanent structures; for example, in Nigeria there is the National Arts Theatre. Such architectural structures exist in many other African countries among them Senegal, Guinea, Kenya and Ethiopia. With this kind of structure stage design on the elaborate scale can be found in their theatrical performances.

The problem of what to collect, catalogue and preserve arose from the following:

(a) Lack of the concept of permanence in staging by the artists themselves. The lack of a general theoretical framework on the essence of stage design both in concept and practice. Immediately a play or a show has ended, the stage is dismantled.

(b) Lack of institutional or governmental support for the theatres in the provision of physical buildings and funds for the upkeep of troupes.

(c) Absence of demands by libraries etc. for theatrical materials and artifacts for purposes of recording and preservation. The libraries/museums must exert their own pressures on the artists and art connoisseurs.

Considering therefore the foregoing problems which hinder collection, cataloguing and conservation of materials on the performing arts in Africa, I would like to make the following recommendations. The burden of effective implementation of this would fall squarely on libraries/museums with adequate state support.

There is need to inculcate a new orientation towards the theatre. I strongly recommend the establishment of Museums of the Performing Arts in the various African countries. The Museums should be autonomous with government subventions supplemented with self-generating activities. Statutory duties would include the collection and preservation of materials, artifacts, documents on the various aspects of the performing arts. The library of each museum would be responsible for the upkeep of documents or information in whatever media as far as it is possible. Such materials as photographs on the performing arts should be collected and then disseminated to other parts of the world. It is however important that audio-visual presentation of the theatrical artifacts should be arranged to keep up the spirit of their use in performance. An example of such a Museum is the "Centre for Black Arts and Civilization" in Nigeria established after Festac in 1977.

The museums have a leadership role to play in order to inculcate the new tradition whereby artists are encouraged to willingly deposit manuscripts, photographs, and posters, etc. Accomplishing this would require maintaining a direct link with theatre groups, theatre organizations, government agents and academic institutions of the performing arts. By so doing, the staff of the museums of the performing arts could establish an effective link with such organizations through constant communication. A project of this nature requires financial support and cooperation from the government, various institutions, theatre groups, individual artists and friends of the Arts.

I would also like to encourage the libraries of the various Institutes of African Studies which are research oriented to take active interest in the collection, cataloguing and preservation of documents and various types of information relating the performing arts as an aspect of African history which is vital and must not be neglected. They must maintain a consistent acquisition policy for books, audio-visual materials, journals and other formats. It is essential also that information about the special collection is widely disseminated.

Many African universities now have departments of performing arts. How effectively are their libraries coping with acquisition, cataloguing, preservation and dissemination of materials - books, posters, programmes, costumes relating to their discipline? Is there any consistent acquisition policy? How are those acquired materials preserved? Are these libraries serving effectively the needs of their clientele? Who are those in charge of the libraries? The libraries have to reexamine their roles within their institutions and the society at large.

In the same way as we have the international exhibitions of industrial wares such as the EXPO 77 and NIGERIA TRADE FAIR, there should be a national exhibition on the performing arts in Africa to bring into one focus the present situation of the performing arts in Africa. Such an exhibition will bring to light the diverse contributions of various artists within each country. It will give an opportunity for recounting achievements and may offer a forum for finding solutions to common problems. Catalogues of such an exhibition could be produced for sale to institutions and individuals.

In conclusion I despair of the fact that the policy on collection, cataloguing and preservation of documents and other artifacts of theatrical performances in Africa to prevent them from disappearing is still in the process of being established. It is an urgent need and a significant desire that should attract the interest of all lovers of the theatre and the reservation of its traditions.

FOR FURTHER READING

Burdick, E.B., Hansen, P.C. and Zanger, B. *eds.*
Contemporary stage design. U.S.A. International Theatre Institute of the United States.

'Festac '77'
Nigeria, Africa Journal Ltd., and The International Festival Committee 1977.

IV World Session Theatre of the Nations, July 13-15, 1978 Colloquium on Theatrical Space.

Hartnoll, Phyllis *ed.*
Oxford companion to the theatre 2nd ed. London, O.U.P. 1951, 762-66.

Ogunbiyi 'Yemi.
Drama and theatre in Nigeria: a critical source book Nigeria, 1981.

THE STAGE DESIGN COLLECTION OF THE NATIONAL ARTS CENTRE, OTTAWA, CANADA

By Anthony Ibbotson

Located in Ottawa, the federal capital of Canada, the National Arts Centre opened in June 1969. It has three performance halls: the Opera, Theatre and Studio, in addition to a Salon used for receptions and exhibitions. Each year some 240 attractions covering all the performing arts are offered in 900 performances to an annual audience of over 700,000.

These attactions are presented by the Centre's four programming departments: Theatre, Music, Dance and Variety and Festival Ottawa - a month long Festival of opera and chamber music. The Theatre Department presents over 30 plays per season in English and French. These may be touring productions from across Canada and abroad, or plays produced by the Centre itself. The Centre has mounted over 160 of its own theatre productions since 1969 and 15 operas since 1971 when the first summer festival was held.

Our stage design collection of over 200 costume and set designs and approximately 100 prop sketches, includes items from virtually all the Centre's own productions. It is constantly growing since, although the costume and set designs are the property of the designer, the Centre is able to purchase a representative selection of designs from nearly every production. A modest collection when compared with that owned by the Metropolitan Toronto Library, it nonetheless, includes works by such leading contemporary Canadian stage designers as Francois Barbeau, Susan Benson, Michael Eagan, Maxine Graham, Brian Jackson, Robert Prévost, Mark Negin and John Ferguson. Designs by Michael Stennett and Robin Fraser Paye from England and the Italian designer, Paolo Ferruzzi also form part of the collection.

We have a video recording of nearly all our plays and operas, colour photographs of actors in full costume and make-up (taken in an impro-

---

ANTHONY IBBOTSON serves as Archivist of the Stage Design Collection of the National Arts Centre in Ottawa, Canada.

vised studio during an actual performance), production photographs, color photographs of the set, technical drawings and over 70 recently restored set models. Our costume collection, including detailed records of actors' measurements, is extensive. Our set design collection, along with other material at the Centre, presents a fairly complete record of a play or opera.

All these records are invaluable for in-house reference purposes, for research into Canadian theatre and for remounting productions, as has happened with two of our plays and nine of the Centre's operas. This wealth of material is ideal for varied and interesting exhibitions which are now mounted on a regular basis in the Centre by the Archives Department in special showcases designed to our specifications.

All design plates are stored in **acid-free** folders, organized by designer name with a cross reference to the actual production. Each design is recorded according to season and the financial code assigned to that production for accounting purposes, e.g.:

MARK NEGIN	*The Tempest*	7273-101-C1 Prospero
	The Tempest	7273-101-C2 Alonso
PAOLO FERRUZZI	*L'Eventail*	7374-100-SD1 - Set design

A slide and color photographic print exist for each design, reducing physical handling of the original work to a minimum. All designs are now photographed before they are returned to the designer. In this way we have a complete design record of a particular production. This rapidly growing collection is readily available for research purposes. The Archives Department also intends to try and photograph as many designs as possible of previous productions by borrowing them from the designers or from private or public collections. Fortunately locating these designs is made easier by the fact that nearly all the designers are alive and living somewhere in Canada, even if a few are no longer actively working in theatre.

Unfortunately a performing arts archivist is seldom in a position to advise a designer as to the choice of paper. Paper is selected to reflect the mood of the play or simply for reasons of economy. Seldom for its **acid-free** qualities! We are all painfully familiar with the conservation problems posed by designs drawn on the back of paper table napkins or cigarette boxes. The Centre's collection has designs on regular drawing paper, kraft paper and a very delicate Japanese paper. When a design reaches the Archives Department we find that it has often been stuck onto a **matte** using whatever adhesive is handy at the time: candle wax, rubber cement, white office glue or double sided tape. Although we are equipped to carry out only simple conservation work, we have ready access to excellent conservation and restoration facilities in Ottawa.

Consequently all our designs requiring special treatment have been examined by experts. Some examples of these special conservation problems are familiar to all archivisists.

Francois Barbeau designed the costumes for our production in French of *Mme Filoumé* by Edouardo de Fillipo. His design for Domenico is on a coarse strawboard which has been covered with a thick coat of white paint. Candle was was apparently used to adhere the design to a purple acidic matting board. As much of the wax as possible has been removed. However the fabric swatch has been left in place for to attempt to remove it would disfigure the design.

The adhesive used on the back of Janet Logan's design for the puppeteer in *Woyzeck* has left an unsightly stain that fortunately is not visible when the design is viewed from the front. The adhesive has been neutralized but we have been unable to determine what type of glue was used.

As the Centre's stage design collection is a contemporary collection we are in the happy position of being able to contact the designers and discover what paper and adhesives they used. We know that Art Penson allowed the paint he used for the background for his designs for *The Fantasticks* to run first. He then turned the paper upside down before drawing the costume design, thereby simulating the effect and texture of the actual set.

Mark Negin's designs for *The Tempest* (produced at the Centre in 1972-73) posed an intriguing conservation and restoration problem. The paint appears to be flaking in parts, yet conservationists were reluctant to touch the design as it was difficult to determine how the paper had been treated. We subsequently contacted Mark Negin who very generously explained his technique to us. After the design was drawn, the paper was painted over with a mixture of printing oil and turpentine and subsequently spattered with a thicker printing oil. Then he sprayed the paper with a semi-gloss fixative which breaks up the oil and turpentine to create the special background characteristic of his work. The solid areas of the design were then painted in, generally in gouache. A semi-gloss fixative was applied before the design was worked over again with charcoal. This lengthy process created the effect visible in plates. As we can detect no visible deterioration since the designs were drawn, a conservationist's advice was not to touch the design but to examine it every six months.

The National Arts Centre's collection of stage designs is a significant one in Canada in that it is kept and administered by the theatre responsible for commissioning the designs in the first place. Costume designs, set designs and models are essentially working tools for the director and production department. It is fitting that, once the play is over, these designs are looked after by the same organization that caused them to be created.

The modest size of our collection has made it possible to organize it in the most efficient way for our needs and to undertake restoration and conservation of designs where necessary. As the National Arts Centre's stage design collection continues to grow it will become an increasingly important record of the history of the performing arts in Canada.

DESIGN BY MOTLEY: A THEATRE AND COSTUME ARTS COLLECTION

by Melissa Cain and Michael Mullin

In 1981 the University of Illinois at Urbana acquired all the costume and set designs belonging to the English design firm Motley. What follows is an overview of the designers' contribution to theatre history, an account of how the designs came to be at Illinois, and a description of their processing by the University Library.

I. The Design Team Motley

In the twentieth century, theatre design came into its own as a major component of theatre production. The Motley designers were part of a group of young people who revolutionized theatrical production in London during the years between the two World Wars, creating "the New Stagecraft."

"Motley" (as in Shakespeare's phrase "Motley's the only wear") was the name under which three women—Elizabeth Montgomery, Margaret Harris and her sister Sophia—worked. Popularly known as Liz, Percy, and Sophie, they first met in 1922 as art students in London. Eager theatre-goers, they made a hobby—and then a business—of sketching actors and actresses in character and selling their works to the performers on payday. When John Gielgud appeared at the Old Vic, they made drawings of him as Richard, Macbeth and Lear, and shyly brought these to his notice. In his autobiographical *Early Stages* he described them as "three silent and retiring young women in those days, and it was some time before I could get them to speak about themselves in their gentle, hesitating voices." Illustrating the theatre world paid the Motleys only modestly, but by it they developed valuable, even life-long, theatrical contacts.

MELISSA CAIN serves as English, Theatre and Cinema Studies librarian at the University Library of the University of Illinois at Urbana-Champaign. MICHAEL MULLIN is Associate Professor of English at the University of Illinois at Urbana-Champaign, specializing in the study of Shakespeare's plays on stage, film and television.

During the years from 1922 to 1930 the Motleys cautiously entered the London theatre scene. Setting up as costume designers, they took a tiny attic room in Pimlico and hired an old Russian woman to sew for them. The earliest Motley creations were fancy dress clothes and period ball gowns for parties and masquerades, sold through London department stores. They also designed costumes for school plays and for a few of Charles Cochran's popular revues at the London Pavilion.

In those days the Old Vic gave an annual costume ball judged by one of its leading actors. In 1930 the three women decided to enter the competition; John Gielgud was the judge. They swept the field, winning six of the twelve prizes. More importantly, they gained Gielgud's personal admiration and esteem.

On the threshold of international fame as an actor, Gielgud's first chance as a director came in 1931 when he directed *Romeo and Juliet* for the Oxford University Dramatic Society (O.U.D.S.). The Motleys offered to design the costumes and he agreed. This initial association between Gielgud and the Motleys was so successful that they became his designers-in-chief for the next eight years, during which period they emerged as London's leading firm. While in Oxford they met George Devine, then President of O.U.D.S., later to be their business manager and, after 1940, Sophie's husband.

The Motleys preferred to collaborate among themselves, not with other designers. For Gielgud's production of *Richard of Bordeaux* (New Theatre, 1933), they insisted on designing sets as well as costumes. "I can't think how we got the nerve," Liz Montgomery recalled. "We knew absolutely nothing about set designs, yet we arrived, shaking, with our designs." *Richard of Bordeaux* was a smash hit and ran for thirteen months in London. The play was so well-received that, according to Gielgud, people came thirty and forty times to see it. Gielgud, at the age of twenty-eight, was catapulted to fame, and the Motleys were established as designers of the first rank.

Over the next forty-three years, the Motleys (whether working together or individually) helped to develop "the New Stagecraft." In their early years with Gielgud during the 1930s their basic approach evolved; one that they followed even after they began working independently later on.

In the decades before the first World War, the old school designers had held sway in London. These "scene painters," as they called themselves, received program credits for individual scenes, and they undertook to render settings that would appear "real"—even archaeologically correct—for the play's historical period and geographical setting. Costumes too, with some leeway for the vanity of actors, were true to the period. During the years between the wars all that changed.

Gordon Craig and Adolphe Appia, to name only one Englishman and one European, wanted to replace historical realism with poetic expressionism. Instead of being theatrical illustrators, theatrical designers became visual interpreters of the play, and Motley was at the vanguard of the movement.

During the 1920s, they had seen and rejected the old school's "fustiness" and "stuffiness" in scenery and costumes, its visual cliches, and its failure to express the play itself. Yet sometimes an especially distinguished production caught their eye. In Nigel Playfair's imaginative 1920 revival of *The Beggar's Opera,* for instance, Claude Lovat Fraser's design demonstrated to the Motleys a "cleanliness and purity" they found appealing and satisfying. For confirmation of their aesthetic taste, they could look not only to Fraser, but also to the work of other designers practicing the same principles: Robert Edmond Jones, Charles Ricketts, and later Theodore Komisarjevsky. As they worked, they began to fix their own ideas of how to design for the stage.

For Motley, the first responsibility of the designers was to serve the play, the actors, and the directors. Turning away from the fusty antiquarianism of earlier Shakespearean productions or its dowdy successor in the Old Vic's stock wardrobe of doublet, hose, and robes, they sought to capture the style of the play through designs that did not exactly reproduce the clothing and locale of the play, but that suggested its mood and architecture. Along with other designers of their time, the Motleys had rejected traditional painted scenery and changes of scene. Instead, they built three-dimensional permanent sets, and changed the scene by shifts in draperies or lighting. In Gielgud's largely unsuccessful *Merchant of Venice* in 1932 the Motleys drew praise from the London *Times* for a simplified setting that restored the Shakespearean speed and grace often thwarted by traditional theatrical conventions. A tall fluted pillar (which was in fact a curtain), a few railings, a few steps, and a balconied doorway were the only furnishings until a long table was brought in for the trial scene.

Much of what Motley did in this and in their other early London productions, we now take for granted as part of the way Shakespeare ought to be staged. Yet is is worth remembering that they were the innovators who found ways to achieve within a modern theatrical idiom the clarity and celerity scholars attribute to Shakespeare's own Globe. Nor was the early success limited to Shakespeare and the classics. Their *Three Sisters* at the Queen's Theatre in 1938 showed them working gracefully in a highly realistic idiom in collaboration with Michel St. Denis, the French director whose recently founded London Theatre Studio would nurture the next generation of actors and directors.

From the fancy dress ball at the Vic in 1930 to the stellar "Queen's

Season" in 1937-38 when Gielgud and his friends Peggy Ashcroft, Marius Goring, Laurence Olivier, Antony Quayle, Ralph Richardson, and Glen Byam Shaw (among others) ran a nine-month repertory in the West End–in five brief and busy years the Motley team had come into its own. They had designed 50 productions, most of them in London, and they had their own studio, Chippendale's old workshop just off St. Martin's Lane. Their studio became an informal gathering place for young actors. Harcourt Williams remembered it as a place "to sip a cup and hear the passing gossip of the theatre, not tittle-tattle, but workmanlike news. There one may meet stars of both firmaments, poets, artists, and at least one gay, enthusiastic Motley." Unusual among designers, they were involved day by day with the actors and directors.

Also unusually, they personally supervised the making of their sets and costumes. Freed of the quest for historical authenticity, they could experiment with new fabrics–in the *Merchant of Venice* (1938), for instance, they made Shylock's costume out of dish rags. Often they would adapt designs freehand on an inexpensive material like unbleached muslin and then paint them with dyes. For the Motleys the designing and making of period costume may be said to be a wedding between illusion and reality, a compromise between fancy and less lovely fact.

Then came the war and everything changed. Just before it broke out, Gielgud's informal company was in Elsinore, performing *Hamlet* in Kroneberg Castle. In the harbor were German battleships. There was a flap about the displaying of Nazi flags, the actors refusing to perform until they were removed. The closing night party at the castle, culminating in a mock-cermonial dunking in the sea, celebrated the last time Gielgud and the rest would be together as a company. The engagement over; with its closing there ended an era of experimentation and maturation in English theatre. The Motleys, in number, were separated. In 1940, Margaret Harris and Elizabeth Montgomery left for New York to design the Laurence Olivier-Vivien Leigh *Romeo and Juliet* production, Intending to stay only three weeks, they found themselves in New York for the duration of the war. There they designed a dozen or so productions for Guthrie McClintic, George Coulouris and Margaret Webster, their designs for McClintic's *Lovers and Other Friends* (1942) winning *Billboard's* first Donaldson Award for costume design. The war ended, Margaret Harris returned to London, where Sophia had designed several productions during the war years, among them *The Importance of Being Earnest* and *Watch on the Rhine.*

Still calling the work "designs by Motley," Elizabeth Montgomery, now married to the writer Patrick Wilmot, stayed on in New York, where she designed for Broadway musicals, beginning with *Carib Song* (1945) and continuing with the original *South Pacific* (1949), *Peter Pan (1950), Paint Your Wagon* (1951), and *The Most Happy Fella* (1956) as well as occasional straight plays like O'Neill's *Long Day's Journey Into Night* (1956). She designed several ballets for Agnes De Mille, among them *Rodeo* (1942) and productions at the Metropolitan Opera, doing costumes and sets for *Simone Boccanegra* (1959) and *Il Trovatore* (1961). In classic plays, Elizabeth Montgomery worked principally with the American Shakespeare Festival in Stratford, Connecticut, designing eight productions from 1957 to 1962, among them *The Merchant of Venice* (1957) starring Katharine Hepburn and *Macbeth* (1961) starring Jessica Tandy.

Back in London after the war; Margaret Harris joined director Glen Byam Shaw in 1946 for a production of *Antony and Cleopatra* at the Old Vic, thereby beginning a fruitful collaboration that would extend over the next dozen years with him there and at the Shakespeare Memorial Theatre in Stratford-upon-Avon. Together, she designed and he directed 12 Shakespeare plays. At the same time, Motley were designing modern plays for George Devine's English Stage Company at the Royal Court Theatre, a showcase for such "angry" young English playwrights as John Osborne, whose premiere production of *Look Back in Anger* (1956) Motley designed.

Even as Sophia and Margaret Harris thrived as designers in London and Stratford, so too the Motley influence among up-and-coming young artists grew. Beginning with the London Theatre Studio founded by St. Denis before the war; the Motley team, and especially Margaret Harris, contributed to efforts to found an English school of theatre design. Immediately after the war, the idea flourished as the Old Vic School and the Young Vic acting company, reappearing in different guise in the early 60s under Margaret Harris' direction as The Design Course of the English National Opera, a school that flourishes today, having recently moved from the ENO workshops in Aldgate to the Riverside Studios in Hammersmith. This involvement in the training of young designers has ensured that Motley's influence continues beyond their own work stage productions. In the work of such students as Jocelyn Herbert, Malcolm Pride, Alan Tagg, Abdul Farah, and Hayden Griffen, a new generation of "Motley" designers has risen to the first rank at the English National Opera, at the National Theatre, at Covent Garden, and at the Royal Shakespeare Theatre, as well as in the West End commercial theatre and abroad.

II. The Motley Collection of Costume and Set Design: Contents and Access

Michael Mullin came upon the Motley designs by a happy combination of research and serendipity. In 1977 in London, he met and interviewed Margaret Harris about Motley's collaboration during the 1950s with director Glen Byam Shaw at Stratford-upon-Avon. He suggested that Margaret Harris and Elizabeth Montgomery gather together all the designs they still possessed to use as the basis for a book on their career. The book has yet to be written, but, by 1980, the designs had been assembled. The Motleys had decided to sell them through Sotheby's. In April of the next year, after complex negotiations, the University of Illinois at Urbana-Champaign purchased the collection.

In September 1981, two large steamer trunks arrived in the University's Rare Book Room, accompanied by Sophie Harris's niece Harriet Jump. Inside these two treasure chests were over 3,400 original Motley items–costume designs, set sketches, notes, photographs, prop lists, story boards and even swatches of fabric. In short, the trunks contained a stunning design archive representing over 150 productions in England and America. here, in one archive, the student and the researcher may find scene renderings and costume designs from a large selection of the Motley's work in plays, operas, and musicals. Spanning four decades of Motley designs, the collection begins in 1932 with Gielgud's *Merchant of Venice* and ends in 1976 with the English National Opera's *Tosca.* Every kind of drawing appears, from rough pencil sketches to final workshop plates. Most designs are in gouache, poster paints or crayola, and some have samples of fabric attached. As fascinating as the drawings themselves are the designer's instructions to the workshop, pencilled on the margins of the drawings.

The cataloguing, classification and storage of the Motley collection, organized by the library and theatre faculty, reflects the practical needs of the users. An early suggestion that the drawings be sorted by size was rejected because it was believed most researchers would need easy access to renderings for specific productions. For this reason the drawings were grouped chronologically, production-by-production, each production taking a general identification/inventory number–a set of digits representing the year, month, and day that the production first opened. (The production of *Henry V,* for example, has the identification number of 510130. The cataloguing was aided in many instances by the Motleys' own pencilled indentifications on the drawings.

The Motley Collection is stored in a humidity-controlled environment in the stack area of the Library's Rare Book Room. As shown in the illustrations, the storage boxes have been labeled on the top and the bottom with the inventory number of the production, the name of the theatre where the production first opened, and, if more than one box was required to store a production, the number of the box in the series.

As yet, only basic conservation measures have been applied to the collection. As the drawings were unpacked from the steamer trunks, they were removed from the plastic folders, flattened out, and when easily done, stripped of rusted pins, staples, and tape. Those drawings that showed mold growing on the edges were disinfected. Increased conservation efforts are planned—the drawings that receive greatest use will be mounted in acid-free mattes and thin tissue will be placed on the top of the matte to keep light and dust from each piece.

Once the renderings were sorted by productions, designs for each production were sub-divided into three categories: costume designs, set designs, and miscellaneous. An inventory sheet for each production was prepared, and individual designs were placed in uniform-size acid-free folders, stored in turn in acid-free boxes. Each folder was marked with the inventory number assigned to the production, followed by the sequential number given the rendering within the production group. In addition, each rendering was itself marked with the numbers which correspond to those on the folder in which it was stored. Accordingly, in these storage boxes the costume designs are found first, then the set designs, followed by miscellaneous materials such as prop drawings, production notes, and plans.

The costume designs were put into four basic groups: designs for principal actors, designs for males, for females, and, finally, designs for broad classes of people (such as soldiers or peasants). Whether male or female, renderings for the principal actors come first, with all designs for a particular character placed in sequential order depending on the act and scene where the costume appeared. In this way, for instance, all costume renderings for *Antony and Cleopatra* in the 1953 production are conveniently grouped together.

The set designs that follow are arranged consecutively in the order they appeared in the play. Often the drawings were not identified by the Motleys as to act and scene, and the cataloguers had to make educated guesses as to what part of the play a drawing represented.

Each rendering in the collection was measured, its artistic medium identified, and, where possible, the character or scene named. All this information appears on the inventory list within each box, and a copy of the inventories are kept in a ring binder in the Rare Book Room for easy reference, providing, in effect, a detailed book catalogue of the collection's contents organized by production. This catalogue has not yet been reproduced although relevant portions of it are available to researchers upon request. The library's ultimate goal is to merge the information recorded in the book catalogue with other significant production information (such as the production's director, choreographer, lighting designer) and thereby to create a full bibliographic record for each rendering. These records will be entered on OCLC, a national computer cataloguing system, providing national access to the Motley collection and introducing such helpful search capabilities as cross-references between the name of the actor and the character role. At present, some OCLC records have been created but most of the collection is not represented in OCLC.

A separate researcher's handlist describes generally the contents of the Motley collection by listing each production year-by-year (as well as the playwright, director and theatre), and indicating the total number of costume designs (CD), set designs (SD) and miscellaneous renderings found for each production.

Not only will the Motley Theatre and Costume Arts Collection benefit scholars working in twentieth-century American and English theatre history, it will also provide a valuable recource for teaching in professional theatre programs. It is hoped that the Motley Collection will serve as a centerpiece for a growing collection of rare and special theatre materials in the University of Illinois Library, especially representative examples of the work of other designers.

I. Costume design by Janet Logan for "The Puppeteer" in *Woyzeck,* the National Arts Centre, Ottowa.

II. Costume design by Art Penson for "Bellamy" in *The Fantasticks,* the National Arts Centre, Ottowa.

III. Costume design by Mark Negrin for "Prospero" in *The Tempest*, the National Arts Centre, Ottowa.

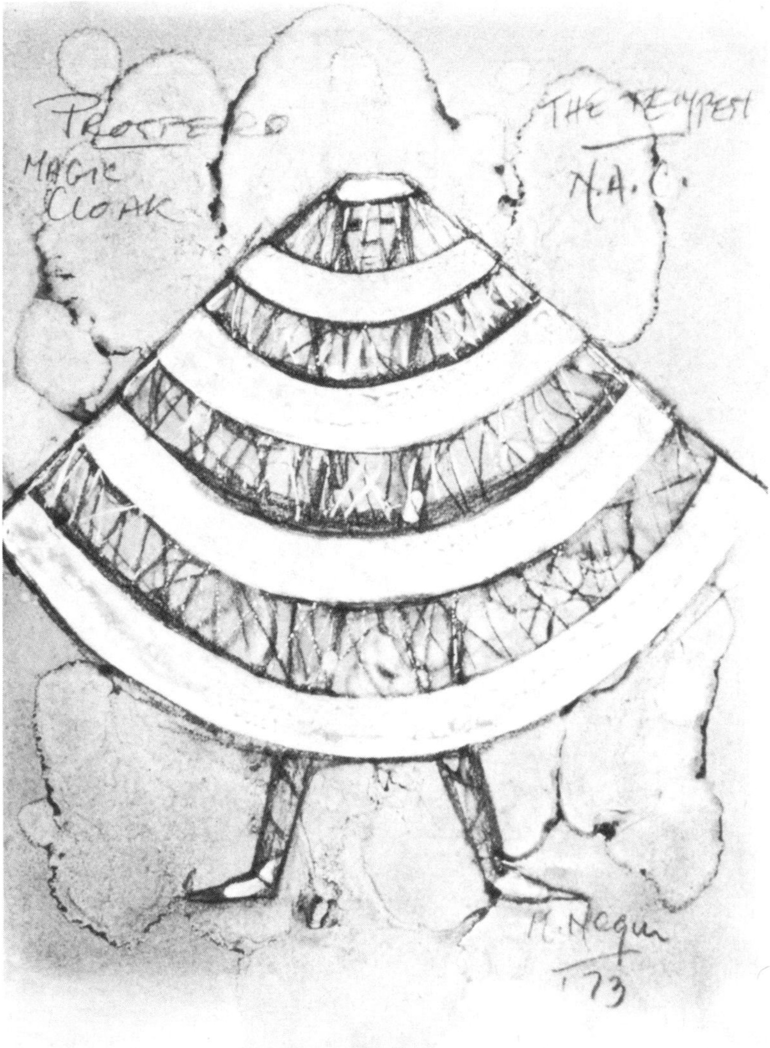

IV. Costume design by Mark Negrin for "Prospero" in *The Tempest,* the National Arts Centre, Ottowa.

V. Costume design by Motley for *Henry V,* with labeled acid-free folder, University of Illinois.

VI. Set design by Stanislav Beložanski for *Simonida* (National Opera, Beograd, 1958), photographed by Hristifor Nastasić for the Museum of Theatre Art, Beograd, Yugoslavia

VII. Set design by Miomir Denić for *Necista KRV* (National Theatre, Beograd, 1975), photographed by Steva Bogdanović for the Museum of Theatre Art, Beograd.

VIII. The Ludwigsburg Court Theatre auditorium, as reconstructed in 1812.

THE MCDOWELL RESEARCH CLASSIFICATION SYSTEM FOR THE CATALOGUING OF SCENE AND COSTUME DESIGNS

by Alan Woods

In cataloguing documents of stage design, a research collection faces some distinct problems. While most collections use the obvious author and title route, designs pose difficulties; frequently, particularly for designs from before the nineteenth century, play titles are not known. Equally frequently, designs bear little obvious connection with the plays for which they are designed. Most importantly, the standard author-title index offers little assistance to the researcher more interested in matters of design styles, or to the practicing modern designer searching for models and for sources on which to base contemporary design work. Possible solutions for those problems were faced by Dr. John H. McDowell and his associates in the Ohio State University Theatre Research Institute (originally Theatre Collection) over thirty years ago. Since the system they devised has been in daily use since then, it would seem to offer a model of potential value.

McDowell's Research Classification System is unique among taxonomies intended for use in theatre collections in that it is firmly based in an iconographic approach. As a system developed for use at a single institution, it contains some idiosyncracies—most notably in its geographic category (element five on the chart), in which the numbers assigned to countries indicate McDowell's own perception of that country's importance to theatrical history. Thus Italy, number one, was in McDowell's estimation much more likely to receive scholarly attention than Ireland, number 30, or all of South America, number 25. Despite these—and other—idiosyncracies, however, the McDowell approach works well as an arbitrary system for pictorial materials.

For stage designs, the McDowell system provides two separate classifications, under "C," costume, and "S," scene design. Individual code numbers, (listed as element four,) then separate design materials

---

ALAN WOODS is the Director of the Theatre Research Institute of the Ohio State University.

according to each design's dominant feature; McDowell provided a manual that carefully defined each number. For example, the manual defines subtopic twenty, "SUBTERRANEAN," as

> –natural or man-made underground areas. Examples: caves, caverns, grottos, tunnels, mine tunnels, sewers, subways, catacombs. Period designs often have a series of concentric wings with connected borders. High rock formations at sides and overhead with open vista in the rear. Long vistas within a grotto. Sometimes a grotto is located upstage with rocks, etc., in foregound. Disqualifying: devils and fire effects (classify as subtopic 11, HELL), or under water (classify as subtopic 1, AQUATIC).

The actual catalogue cards have space for more than one code for a single design, thus permitting cross-classification; if the design plate includes, costumed figures, for example, the costume designs can be catalogued along with the scene design. This built-in cross-reference system allows great freedom to the cataloguer, and provides multiple entry points for the user into the classification system.

The McDowell catalogue, moreover, is not limited solely to the codes presented on the chart; additional catalogues exist for the theatrical artist involved with the material, the theatre with which the material is associated (if known), and the title of the performance piece for which the design was intended. Another catalogue is provided for material, whether iconographic or textual, pertaining to the characters of the *commedia dell'arte*. This existence of this last catalogue is another example of the personal idiosyncracies of a catalogue system created by a single person–Professor McDowell was particularly interested in the *commedia* form, devoting annual seminars to the subject; hence the emphasis placed on the masks of the *commedia*.

The various cross-referenced catalogues have specific and valuable uses. The Research Classification Code, obviously, groups together material of similar subject matter; to use our previous example of subtopic 20, "SUBTERRANEAN," the code provides information on all material which has been catalogued–and like most collections, those of the Theatre Research Institute are not fully catalogued, although a separate catalogue (to be discussed later) does provide a rough means of accessing uncatalogued items. The initial element in the code is a chronological descriptor; thus, at catalogue section F S D 20, one finds all entries for scene designs having a predominantly subterranean motif, originally intended for ballet or court dance and dated to the half century between 1650 and 1699, while at F S E 20, similar designs for plays or operas can be located. In addition to being grouped chronologically and by branch of entertainment, the "SUBTERRANEAN" scene designs are filed together by country of origin.

The benefits of this approach should be obvious: through cataloguing by subject matter, it becomes possible for the user to have access to all materials with similar subjects, thus permitting comparisons. It is also possible, as many of our graduate students have done in research projects, to trace the treatment of specific scenic subjects over an extended period of time, in order to demonstrate how changing theatrical conventions and technical capabilities affect the ways in which designers treat the same subject. Cross-national comparisons are also possible, although for example, in the seventeenth and eighteenth centuries, the international influence of Italian designers somewhat lessens the value of such comparisons. For later periods, however, this has proved a fruitful area of research.

While the Research Classification System groups together like materials, the various cross-reference catalogues provide other ways for the user to approach the materials in the files. One of the designs from the second half of the seventeenth century catalogued under subtopic 20, "SUBTERRANEAN," for example is a design by Ferdinando Tacca for the 1661 Florence production of *Ercole in Tebe,* from an engraving held by the Biblioteca Nazionale Braidense in Milan. It is the only work by Tacca with this particular code. Using the "Artist" catalogue, however, the researcher can easily locate all other designs by Tacca which have been catalogued by the Institute's staff. Similarly all other designs for *Ercole in Tebe* are filed together in the "Play" catalogue. Similarly, the "Theatre" catalogue permits the researcher to examine all materials associated with a specific theatre.

As mentioned earlier, the Ohio State University Theatre Research Institute, like most theatre collections, is woefully behind in the process of cataloguing materials already acquired. The reasons are the same as those elsewhere: low levels of funding mandate an extremely small staff. At Ohio State, the normal problems are compounded by the fact that our staff is composed entirely of students; the Theatre Research Institute, unlike other collections, exists primarily as a resource for the students in our training programs, although other researchers do make use of the collected materials. As result, there is a constant turnover of staff, with most student assistants remaining for only two or three years; the perpetual turnover means constant training. Due to this problem, which has existed since the founding of the Institute in 1950, Professor McDowell and his assistants devised a holding catalogue into which all materials are entered upon acquisition. The holding catalogue—essentially an Author, Title, Subject listing—does allow the user to locate material, but does not provide the extensiv cross-indexing nor the iconographic locators which are the strength of the Research Classification System. Although woefully inadequate, the holding catalogue does at least permit rough access to material.

A further strength of the Institute's holdings lies in McDowell's decision, in 1950, to concentrate on the acquisition of microforms rather than the purchase of actual material. In the 1950s and 1960s particularly, when the American dollar was relatively strong against European currencies, this made the acquiring of large amounts of material on relatively limited budgets possible. A rough estimation of the Institute's current holdings is that approximately 450,000 frames of microfilmed documents, including designs, scripts, prompt-books, and manuscripts, are in the archives. The majority of these have been acquired from over one hundred museums and libraries, primarily in Europe. As an example, using the same scene design subtopic as before, "SUBTERRANEAN:" some 38 designs from the first half of the nineteenth century have been catalogued. The original designs are held by the Museo della Scala, the Biblioteca Nazionale Braidense, the Uffizzi Gallery, and the Biblioteca Nazionale Marciana in Italy; the Victoria and Albert Museum, Islington Central Library, and the British Museum in England; the Toneel Museum in Amsterdam; the Nationalbibliothek in Vienna; and the Library of Congress, the collections of the Cooper Union, the Huntington Library, and the Donald Oenslager Collection in the United States. The microform collection thus makes it possible for the researcher to examine materials from widely separated collections, providing a significant economic saving to the student, as research trips to Europe can be focused by extensive work prior to actual travel.

The McDowell Research Classification System code, when taken in conjunction with its several cross-referenced catalogues, provides a useful model to consider, particularly since the system has been in use since its development in the early 1950s and has had an influence on later efforts to establish classification schemes for theatrical materials. Most notably, the chronological and geographic framework was adapted by Frederick M. Litto for his *American Dissertations on the Drama and the Theatre* (1969), which in turn has served as the basis for the annual bibliography of American dissertations in progress published in *Theatre Journal* (formerly *Educational Theatre Journal).*

What are the system's major flaws? Apart from the personal biases most clearly expressed in the geographic category, the system's most serious drawback is the lack of a subject category for textual materials, which are lumped together under each topic with the use of asterisks defined in the manual as "no subcategory." Although there are subcategories under topic "P," "Play," those subtopics separate textual materials by type of publication rather than by other considerations—genres are not recognized, for example. Under topic "A," "Artist," the system does not permit differentiation among biography, autobiography, or critical analysis. The system precludes, in short, any precise categorization of purely textual material. While it works extremely well for pictorial material, it does not work at all for the textual. This limitation was recognized by Professor McDowell and his associates, who created the holding catalogue to fill that particular gap. There does not exist, however, any standard set of classifications for the holding catalogue, with the result that its subject entries vary widely, cataloguing having been done over a thirty-year period by a succession of student assistants lacking any training in such matters.

For iconographic materials, most particularly for scene and costume designs, theatre plans, and technical drawings, however, the Research Classification System developed by Professor McDowell functions well. Once the definitions of the subtopics are understood, it is extremely easy to access all pertinent material within the Institute's rich holdings and, as does any competent scheme for cataloguing, the system not only makes availability relatively painless, but suggests research topics as well. While it is not perfect, it does provide a starting point, particularly for the classification of material which is primarily visual.

MASTER CHART–RESEARCH CLASSIFICATION SYSTEM

1	2	3	4
A. to 200 BC	A. ARTIST	A. Cinema	*
B. 199 BC to 499	C. COSTUME	B. Circus C. Commedia	1. Contemporary Dr. 2. Contemporary Uniform or Prof. 3. Non-Contemp. Dress 4. Non-Contemporary Uniform or Prof. 5. Fantastic 6. Bird or Animal 7. Mask
C. 500 to 1499	L. LIGHTING	D. Dance	1. Instrument 2. Control Equip. 3. Accessory 4. Planning or Design
D. 1500 1599 E. 1600 to 1649	M. STAGING	E. Legitimate F. Mechanical Theatre	1. Flying Mach. 2. Raising Mach. 3. Lateral Mach. 4. Revolving Mach. 5. Special Effect 6. Scenery 7. Stage Equipment 8. Shop Equipment, Material or Painting
F. 1650 to 1699	P. PLAY	G. Pageants	1. Standard script 2. Non-Standard script 3. Musical script 4. Scenario 5. Program 6. Playbill or Poster
G. 1700 to 1749 H. 1750 to 1799 I. 1800 to 1849 J. 1850 to 1899	S. SCENE DESIGN	H. Television I. Non-Theatrical J. Satirical Print	1. Aquatic or Shipboard 2. Air or Land Transportation 3. Business or Trade 4. Castle or Fortification 5. Church or Temple 6. Civic or Governmental 7. Cloud or Celestial 8. Domestic 9. Factory or Heavy Industry 10. Garden or Park 11. Hell 12. Landscape, Wood or Mountain 13. Non-Localized Scenic Units 14. Palace 15. Place of Burial 16. Place of Entertainment 17. Procession or Parade 18. Professional & Educational 19. Public square, Street or Roadway 20. Subterranean 21. Tent
K. 1900 to 1949 L. 1950 to	T. THEATRE		1. Stage or Auditorium 2. Entire Building 3. Facade, Building or Grounds 4. Foyer or Adjacent Public Area 5. Administrative or Technical Service Area

5	
Africa	22
Albania	13
Asia Minor	14
Atl. Isles	37
Australia	36
Austria	5
Belgium	7
Bulgaria	28
Canada	31
C. America	32
China	42
Czech.	16
Denmark	19
E. Indies	27
England	3
Finland	23
France	2
Germany	4
Greece	9
Holland	6
Hungary	18
India	39
Ireland	30
Italy	1
Japan	24
Korea	26
Med. Isles	33
Mexico	40
N. Zealand	34
Norway	11
Pac. Isles	38
Poland	20
Portugal	35
Roumania	41
Scotland	44
S. America	25
S. E. Asia	45
Spain	21
Subarctic	46
Sweden	10
Switzerland	8
Unknown	0
U.S.A.	12
U.S.S.R.	15
Wales	43
W. Indies	29
Yugoslavia	17

PROBLEMS AND OBSERVATIONS CONCERNING THE TRANSLATION OF SCENOGRAPHIC TERMS FROM FRENCH TO ENGLISH

by Alfred S. Golding

The preparation of the English text for the Third Edition of *Performing Arts Libraries and Museums of the World* has afforded me the privilege of participating with learned colleagues from many countries in a significant cooperative scholarly endeavor. I know that I do not speak only for myself when I declare that all of us who have taken part in this undertaking are particularly grateful to Professor André Veinstein for his resolute and wise leadership in bringing this effort to fruition. Once again the world of theatre scholarship is in his debt.

The past four years in which I have been involved in this collaboration have provided me with an opportunity to view in fresh perspective the language which we as performing arts practitioners and scientists customarily employ in our professional lives. Like other technical languages, that of the performing arts is a repository of usage both old and new, of meanings accreted and shifted, of nomenclature applied broadly and narrowly. The imperative of capturing word sense precisely and of nicely conforming French and English idiom, has made me acutely sensitive to the semantic nuances in the technical verbage of both languages–distinctions which by their very commonality tend to escape our professional notice. It is an inescapable truism that the words of one language do not always match another. This is even the case with so technical a vocabulary as that of the theatre where homologues (cognates having a common classical root) are shared by many languages. Yet the use of a common analagous term shared by French and English may not necessarily prove accurate because the technical object or process to which the term makes reference may itself differ from country to country. The translation problem is further complicated when (except for informants in French-and English-speaking countries), respondents to our original questionnaires have

---

ALFRED S. GOLDING serves as Professor of Theatre History at the Ohio State University in Columbus, Ohio.

had to translate information from their native language into French or English, and this version, after redaction, has had to be translated once again into either French or English. Additional difficulties are posed when western languages become the vehicle for conveying performance practices found in non-western cultures. Fortunately for the translator, during the past century performing arts nomenclature has tended to become more standardized throughout the world. This general trend, in all probability, has been accelerated during the past three decades by the formation of international theatre research organizations such as ITI, IFTR and SIBMAS. This notwithstanding, the problem of corresponding terms becomes doubly complicated when historical terminology is employed which has retained its original meaning at the same time that it has acquired a second variant. Today I wish to present for your attention several instances of these translating difficulties, as well as some general observations on the nature of theatrical language. Since the focus of this conference is upon scenography, I shall confine my remarks to this area, although similar linguistic phenomena may be as readily observable with regard to performance and non-scenic glossaries.

My first point is that the "Blue Book" *(Performing Arts Libraries and Museums)* is not merely a register of information about performing arts collections but a record of growth and change in scenic form and technique as well. That record is encapsulated in the very language in which scenic artists articulate their views to fellow practitioners, and which language curators and bibliographers inevitably pick up and utilize for their scenographic indexes. Seen from this point of vantage, the three editions of the "Blue Book" in themselves constitute historic documents which reveal tendencies towards change and continuity in scenographic usage. If, for the sake of example and brevity, we confine our observation to the present edition we will find still persisting terms of long theatrical tradition such as *décor scenique* – "stage decoration" – placed alongside the more recent *éclairage,* which in current usage has come to mean not only "lighting," but "the art of stage lighting." Or, we will discover the existence of early techniques of dress design which require the dressmaker to use *enchantillons de tissu* – "fabric samples" – to conform the costume to the specifications of the designer. That term, arising from early dressmaking practice can be found in the "Blue Book" beside *animation,* of recent coinage, a word identical in meaning in both French and English and having reference to the technique of photographing cartoon drawings in sequential action so that they seem to move in motion picture projection. Similarly, the hoary architectural *plan technique*–technical drawing in plan – or the equally traditional mode of reproducing architectural drawing by plate photography – *cliche verre*–are terms which have their modern counterpart in the very recent method of reproducing drafting plates from drawings originally made on clear plastic sheeting so as to create "Mylar copy," as it is known in the American copyright version of the process.

In addition to technical nomenclature of theatrical provenance, the Third Edition reveals the presence of terms both old and new which derive from scholarly and curatorial usage. With respect to performance documentation alone, several prominent examples may be cited. Thus while *dessins originaux* – "the original designs of the artist" and *photographies* and *diapositives* –"photographs" and "color slides" – previously had been major iconographic means of reconstructing the appearance of a setting or costume during the course of performance, the increased incidence of new terms like *enregistrements, video, bandes magnetiques* and *cassettes* reflect the innovative employment of the motion picture and the television camera to record the sight as well as the sound of stage presentation. Counterpoised against age-old methods of scenic projection using light and shadow effect, exemplified in the Levantine Karaghoz and the European *laterna magica,* are such current marvels as the *ombre magique,* listed among the holdings of the National Museum of Technology at Prague, and the sophisticated motion picture apparatus which are identified as part of the collections of numbers of museums of cinematography.

The latest edition of *Performing Arts Libraries and Museums* also contains a record of the vocabulary employed to designate the artifacts which are created as by-products of scenery-making. We may recognize the rough sequence of that process in works like *esquisse de décor, croquis technique,* the aforementioned *dessin, plan technique, elevation technique,* and *maquette plane* and *maquette construite.* Thereby we are aware that the set designer, working independently or following the instructions of the *regisseur,* prepared a "rough sketch" of a prospective scene, then fashioned a more exact but still "unfinished preliminary drawing" of the stage picture to be shown to the director for approval. From these terms we further learn that the designer, following the acceptance of the "drawing," prepared a finished color "rendering" either in the form of a "perspective picture" or a "three-dimensional model" of the stage set. On the basis of this depiction or construction, the scenic artist thereafter produced "ground plans," "side and sectional elevations" (for the carpenter and the painter) and additional final "technical drawings" for building and painting especially difficult pieces of scenery.

While most words in the French and English scenographic lexicon can be firmly paired, a few may be found which defy ready matching and which therefore present problems for the translator. A case in point is the nearly ubiquitously utilized *mise en scène.* At least to the nineteenth century, the word was used in its general literal sense as the placement of actors and scenic background upon a stage. Subsequently in the late nineteenth and early twentieth centuries, the meaning of the term became more focused, so as to convey the idea of a production mounted in a unified artistic manner according to the views of Appia and other stage designers. In recent years the sense of *mise en scène* as a scheme of design by which all production elements–visual and audial, scenographic and histrionic–are coordinated has become dominant, particularly among theatre practitioners. But something of the original sense is still present, for we may discover that some archivists use the term as a referent for scenery created by a designer, rather than for the production design as a whole. Perhaps the use of *mise en scène* as "setting" has been retained because, after all, that is its literal meaning. Or perhaps it continues in the lexicon because the scenographic record offers visual proof of the fact that a production has been designed according to artistic principles and therefore is in a form which is readily recognizable. Be that as it may, depending upon the context and supplementary information supplied by our informants, the term has been translated in either of two ways: if the term occurs as a record of the design activity of the *regisseur* it is rendered as "directorial conception;" if it occurs as evidence of the activity of the scenic artist it is translated as "stage design."

I have in great part here (as with certain other problems in translating terms of variant meaning) relied upon Patrice Pavis' *Dictionnaire du théâtre: termes et concepts de l'analyse.* For further discussion of the term, see Professor André Veinstein's *La Mise en scène théâtrale et sa condition aesthetique,* 1955.

A similar difficulty of translating scenographic referents which have retained both a general and a specific or technical designation is encountered in words like *artisanat* and *meubles.* When used in their broad sense they can be found quite apart from a theatrical milieu, where they may regularly signify, respectively, "arts and crafts" and "furniture." But each also has a specific performing arts application. Thus, *artisanat* is occasionally found in vocabulary of the performing arts curator, where it indicates "theatrical properties," particularly that smaller variety which the actor carries and manipulates in the hand. Hence it has been translated by the equally technical term of "hand properties." So also we may note that in the "Blue Book" the word *meubles* is employed in an exact theatrical context to mean the tables, chairs and other furniture which are used to dress a stage set. hence it is rendered by "set furnishings" unless the reference is to the furniture of an artist's room which has become part of the holdings of a theatre museum. In the latter case the word is rendered in its general sense.

By way of conclusion we may take note that the "Blue Book" in its

Third Edition is not merely a repository of information about scenographic documentation, but also about the form such materials take and how they are gathered, catalogued and preserved in performing arts libraries and museums of the world. So we may discover that the evidence of the art of the scene and costume designer is available for study in *documents iconographiques*–"iconographic documents"–principally comprising *peintures, portraits, tableaux, estampes, gravures,* and *figurines*–"paintings," "portraits," "pictures," "prints," "engravings," and even "figurines," as well as verbal descriptions contained in *coupures de presse*–"press clippings" and *registres de comte*–"account books," in addition to the previously cited new "recording" modes –*enregistrements*– using videotape and motion picture film. These sources usually have been acquired, according to our informants, *des achats* and *des dons*– "by purchase and gift" but seemingly never, as are published plays by national libraries, *en depôt* – "for copyright deposition." Our informants round the world tell us, furthermore, that scenographic documentation may be preserved in *albums,* or found in *receuils de presse, dossiers,* or *cabinets des dessins* and *cabinets des estampes*– "press or paper files" and "drawing and print archives." There they may be incorporated within an institution's larger holdings or kept intact, in this latter instance designated as *restées* (or *conservées) groupées.* Information about such holdings may be obtained through published catalogues or in "card files" –*fichiers*–invariably systematically organized as a *catalogue raisonné,* according to *auteurs, matières* and (sometimes) *titres.* We are also informed that performing arts catalogues may be connected by "cross-reference" – *liens méthodiques* with other catalogues within and without the library or museum, with each item detectable by its special *côte* or call numbers or letters.

SOME EXPERIENCE IN COLLECTION OF DOCUMENTS ON THEATRE SCENERY FROM THE PAST

by Olga Milanovic

When we received the task of maintaining the collection of sketches for scenery in the Serbian Museum of Theatre Art (Belgrade, Yugoslavia), we were faced with numerous problems. First of all, the specific development of the Serbian theatre, which gradually became professional by the middle of the nineteenth century, and developed intensively in the spirit of the European classical theatre, promoting at the same time its own, largely folk tradition, represented a specific challenge. Our ambition has been both to determine the continuity of this art, and to find the original forms of Serbian scenography. Unfortunately, our history has been full of wars - liberating ones during the last century, and unifying ones in this century. The two world wars of this century almost completely destroyed the results of theatre development in Serbia.

Our efforts to collect the original sketches of scenery from the eighteenth and nineteenth centuries have been so hampered that we have placed our main accent on collecting and publishing monographs and historical works on this field during the three decades since our museum has been established. We aim to bring into light the work of those lone artists who were pioneers in the struggle to liberate our stage from stereotyped copying of standard productions from European theatre centers. The most difficult task has been to establish a creative link with theatric performances at a time distance, varying from a few decades to over one century.

Critical reviews of first-night performances have been the most important connection between the preserved sketches for scenery and the resulting theatre achievements. Data on the performance, given in these reviews, provided the possibility for discerning the orientation of directing and its relation to scenography, the importance of stage design in the accomplishment of a director's ideas, harmony or dis-

---

OLGA MILANOVIC serves as Scientific Advisor to the Serbian Museum of Theatrical Art in Belgrade, Yugoslavia.

harmony with directing, consistency of style and esthetic values. The scenographer's activities in different subsequent productions, and the determination of characteristic features of individual accomplishments, affinities and mutual relations among all artists-creators of a performance, gave insight into the developing stages of scenery achievements—deeply individual and creative, in spite of numerous limitations and eclectic styles. The analysis of the artistic genesis of scenery pointed out the distinctive manuscript of the stage designer—his education, techniques that he applied, ideals that he wanted to reach, his originality, as well as his adaptability to numerous problems faced within relations with the director. Finally, the results of scenery had to be determined - from the original idea up to the final achievement. This arduous work required a lot of patience, but it led to the possibility of understanding wholly and objectively the completed work of the stage designer. This kind of research had to follow traces of the forgotten performances and stage masters who were forerunners of modern stage designers, and have been based upon painstaking methods of reconstruction of past theatre performances.

What is the role of the theatre critic in this system of evaluation? In the period between the two world wars, and that after the liberation of Yugoslavia, numerous writers and journalists of renown wrote theatre reviews for publication in both literary and theatre magazines. They threw light on many different esthetic and ideological aspects of productions. Every critical review is always important, under the condition that it is not based exclusively upon the literary analysis of the play. However, reviews treating the stage performance, in analysis of certain component parts or of the play as a whole, usually represent the key for understanding the visual element of stage design. Although the reviews, most often, contain only a few phrases on the stage design, there are cases when a constructive approach can be found, as well as the role of scenery in the general achievement of the play. By comparing the opinions of several critical observations or particular analyses of the complete performance, objective conclusions may be drawn on scenography as a specific form of art.

Another question could be raised in this connection—is the stage design information in a review partial or independent in relation to the performance as a whole? If this is not the case, should greater attention be devoted to mise-en-scene, so that the review, besides its evaluation of the performance, should contain stage design analysis in more detail? We emphasize this question as it is so vitally topical even today. The issue has been very important for historical research of the past, but today - when the art of scenery is in the forefront of the struggle for a modern theatre expression - it is even more important, and even decisive.

CONSERVING THEATRE DESIGNS FOR THE RECORD AND FOR EXHIBITION: A DESIGNER'S VIEWS.

by Peter T. Vagenas

Designers for the theatre do not, traditionally, create their works of art for exhibit or for posterity; they create their work for live performance with the drawings, sketches, and models serving, most importantly, as a basis for the full scale product rather than for mounting, framing and storing. I will narrow my discussion to focus, generally, on scenic design and allude to costume and lighting design only where appropriate in relation to scenery. Lighting design poses its own peculiar set of problems and the challenge of conserving and exhibiting costumes sets up problems similar to those of scenic design, but much less complex.

Exhibitions mounted by the United States Institute for Theatre Technology and its international institute for the Prague Quadriennial require efforts similar to those required for mounting exhibits of small scale sculptures, and must be planned years in advance. Designers who wish to have their works considered for exhibit often must revive and revise already completed works to conform to the formats required by the exhibitor, to prepare the work which was not originally in an appropriate form for exhibit, and to produce completely fresh sketches or models which were worn from use as tools for communication in conferences with directors, producers, and, at times, with choreographers. A choreographer smashed a rather fragile model I had created while demonstrating the potentials of the setting. The records of theatrical productions, consisting of to-scale drawings, sketches, models, and photographs of these working pieces plus photographs of the actual live performance quite often collect dust in the designer's closet—the work of the moment detracts from the efforts required to keep and store a portfolio which is readily submitted for exhibit. As a graduate fellow at the University of Denver, I had the pleasure of pulling numerous drawings, color elevations, and some rough sketches,

---

Designer PETER T. VAGENAS is Associate Professor of Design and Chairperson of the Department of Theatre at the University of Delaware.

of Robert Edmond Jones from several drawers in a closet adjacent to my basement office. These valuable records, though periodically exhibited, were stored in fashion similar to that which I accord my own, historically insignificant work. The work represents Jones experiences at the Central City Opera House. Jones, apparently, cared little for posterity and had no concern for the potential value of this work to historians, critics, and collectors. With storage space at a premium, the institution took little care in preserving the documents. To its credit, the Central City Opera Association has preserved records of his work there. The collector of design records needs to understand that the live performance provides the only valid experience for the spectator; photographs, sketches, and models are static, rather sterile representations of the designer's artistry.

The record of the designer's work is collected, for the most part, in volumes on the history of theatre and in biographical volumes treating only the most important works of the designer. Few of these volumes deal critically or adequately with the works which are photo-reproduced—poorly too much of the time—providing the researcher with little material in depth with which to appraise the designer's contributions to the art. The static photograph, unaccompanied by exhaustive explication of concepts and achievements of goals in the actual performance, and without the comments of the collaborators, leave the beholder/reader little on which to appraise the work or great lattitude in assuming the substance of the designer's efforts. Filmed or video-recorded performances before live audiences are probably the closest we can come to providing interested folk primary material on which to appreciate and critique the works. The plastic dimension plus the fourth dimension of time are lost forever with the close of the production. Film or tape, though two-dimensional, captures the quality of life, color, sound, and emotion of the performance. The Guggenheim Museum's recent Costakis exhibit and the Hirshhorn's exhibit of last year including full-scale reproductions of settings created for director V. Meyerhold's productions designed by Constructivists were interesting and valuable to the degree that the beholder could appreciate the dynamic of the architecture as the actors would have used them. The non-theatrical environment and the lack of theatrical lighting diminished the impact of these exhibits. Incidently, these reproductions, unadorned by appropriate physical or lighting environments, were probably much more successful as structural architecture than designs of an illusionistic, pictorial form would have been under similar circumstances.

These introductory comments are not designed to suggest that there is no value in conserving and exhibiting "paper" or model records of designs for the theatre. I have simply described the relativity of values and have attempted to explain, from my point of view, the reasons that collecting, maintaining, and exhibiting designers' works is so problematical and the reasons designers do not usually prepare their works for such purposes.

Three volumes with which I am familiar, Robert Edmond Jones, Jo Mielziner, and Donald Oenslager, constitute relatively fine records of these important designers' works. Mielziner's book is particularly valuable since it is a memoir and includes the relatively detailed account of the process which lead to the creation of his designs for Arthur Miller's *Death of a Salesman,* and his personal summary comments about each of the other works contained in the volume. The *Death of a Salesman* project illustrates for us the critical role that collaboration plays in the creation of the work credited to, or blamed on, the designer. This treatise is all the more valuable if the researcher takes the time to study director Elia Kazan's notes and Arthur Miller's accounts of the process which lead to the live performance. Mielziner's beautiful color sketches (he began his career as an easel painter) produced with a fair degree of fidelity in the volume do not, unfortunately, complete the record; good color prints of the actual production are wanted. The designer's sketch represents a greatly simplified, highly focused and impressionistically lighted, complete with costumed characters, dramatic moment in the play. The sketch functions as an element in the communication of concepts to the director, playwright, and other design staff. The photograph of the same moment in performance will almost always be significantly different and needs to be included to complete the graphic display. The enlarged photoprints of the actual performance illustrated together with the full scale model and a color sketch of the concept of A. Popova's setting for the *Magnanimous Cuckold* at the Guggenheim proves my point. The half-inch-to-a-foot model, when expertly done, is, of course, much simpler to deal with in exhibit than a full-scale reproduction. Storage, shipping, maintaining while exhibiting models require floor space, glass cases, and special lighting. Ideally, miniature spotlights, paralleling the original lighting scheme and design, could recreate the mood and architectonic sense of the live performance, particularly if viewed through or in the frame of the to-scale theatre in which the work was produced. The model, color sketches, and photographs of performances plus designers' summaries of concepts would provide a relatively complete view and appreciation of the designers' contribution to the production and his/her artistry. The exhibit would have value for the casual observer as an esthetic entity and as an enlightening view of the designers' place in the theatre. The critic/judge, historian, esthetician, and theatre designer would be provided a comprehensive view of the works. If the designer is living, his own commentary could be recorded for play-back by the spectators. This appears to be the most economical and satisfactory form of presenting design works.

Photographic records of designers' "paper" works and models are relatively easy to produce with quality by the professional who is expert in shooting art works—special lighting, selection of color films which complement the color as well as other elements which the designer is not usually equipped to master. Photographs of the live performance are extremely complex and must be approached with the view that revelation of design elements as well as the performer are paramount for purposes of design records. Lighting contrasts on the stage are exaggerated generally to the degree that photographs taken for the producer or the publicist/promoter usually high-light the performer and allow the scenery to recede into darkness, even when the actual lighting is re-created for the photographic session. The live audience's visual acuity is greater than the camera's and permits him to maintain a visual balance between environmental architecture and performer. Adjustments to the lighting which maintain the appropriate visual sense and esthetic of the original is critical for the record. This precluded the possibility of taking photographs of actual performances—shutter noise is distracting also. A "call" for purposes of photography is costly in the commercial theatre and attempting to serve the diverse needs of the designer, producer, promoter in one session would likely take considerable extra time which would also be cost prohibitive. The limitation of film speed constitutes another problem with "shooting live" which might be feasible during dress rehearsals. Color bias in film, though less critical now than in the past, continues to warp the actual color of scenery, costumes, and lighting on the stage. Some times the best solution is to pose the dramatic moment, to freeze and photograph it with the camera mounted on a tri-pod. This method produces the best photographic resolution and the best opportunity to adjust lighting until colors and contrasts are balanced. The dramatic moment is unsatisfactorily captured according to many of my colleagues who dislike posed photographs. I personally believe that this compromise with spontaneity of live action is acceptable given the benefits for the record. Photographic records of costume designs are simpler and generally, if care is exercised, much more effective than those of scenery. Who can forget the wonderfully expressive portrait of Lady Windermere gowned in Cecil Beaton's creation which, though in black and white communicates quite accurately the elegance and grace of the actual garment in performance.

Slides which are rear-screen projected constitute another form of presentation which, under appropriate environmental lighting conditions, is much more effective than photoprints. This form appears to possess more life and represents the third dimension more forcefully than prints. As a designer, I prefer to present my own and the works of others in this form for the reason stated above and because it is the most efficient and economical means of presenting designs. I assume that mounting a large exhibit in this form would not be possible technologically or economically in museums. As I prepared this paper and thought about projecting an exhibit, I was reminded of the Laterna Magica of the Expo '67 World's Fair in Montreal. In one large space, spectators could surround a four-sided screen complex which is a self-contained tour of the exhibit and could travel rather inexpensively by truck without fear of losing or damaging original works. Such an exhibit could be accompanied by recorded explanations and designers' notes, could mix pictures of live performances and "paper" examples of the design process, and include filmed or video-taped segments of the live performances. Though contact with the actual color sketch or model is absent in such an exhibit, my belief that any static exhibit is far from ideal, leads me to conclude a fuller experience with the performance is valid and desirable.

My research dealing with the Russian Constructivists has been frustrated by the lack of comprehensive and well-produced records. Little has been written by the designers themselves and only a few collectors have accumulated a significant number and range of representative works and photographs of performances. Costakis' collection and the Lobanov-Rostovsky collection are notable exceptions. Herbert Marshall's collection of production photographs is another valuable record of this remarkable movement. The photographs are not very good and the reproductions in books and catalogues diminish the effectiveness of the record even further. Periodicals such as *Theatre Crafts, Lighting Dimensions, Theatre Design and Technology, World Theatre,* to name a few, are creating a valuable record of design production in featuring prominent artists in photographic displays of sketches and performances complemented by interviews describing the process and concepts. A substantial bibliography is accumulating which will be available to all of us and will aid us in locating original sources and materials. The catalogue of designs throughout the world produced by the International Theatre Institute and published in the U.S.A. by Theatre Arts Books constitutes another valuable source for the records. In reviewing the . . . *Since 1960* edition, I complimented the publishers for including a section dealing with the designers' concepts for a number of the unique entries but wished there had been a designer's brief for each of the entries. Though costs would be far greater for this excellent series, I firmly believe that photo production in color for every appropriate entry would make this series far more valuable as a collector's volume and as a source for theatre researchers, critics, and teachers.

Conclusions: Inadequate records due to designers' lack of interest, lack of time, or lack of adequate recources contribute to an inadequate or much less than ideal record for preserving and exhibiting designers' works. The poor quality of photo-reproductions resulting from inadequate equipment or materials, or inexpert photography contributes to the malaise. Educating designers and theatre producers to value their work for posterity will contribute to solving this aspect of the problem. Collectors and exhibitors must take into account the designers' view about what constitutes effective representation of live theatrical performances when exhibited out of the context of the original. The realization that drawings, sketches, and models are only a means to achieve the live performance rather than works of art that stand alone will contribute to improved presentations.

INFLUENCE OF STAGE DESIGN ON MUSIC/DRAMA

by Nadežda Mosusova

An interesting subject was proposed to me by the organizers of the 15th SIBMAS Congress in New York to talk about stage design as exerting influence on music/drama. I took the proposal as a challenge because to view music/drama, whether German, Russian or Yugoslav, from the standpoint of development of scene or stage itself, represents a very unusual approach to the history and theory of opera and to the history and development of ballet music.

Researchers into the history and esthetics of opera, in principle, hardly ever touch upon the visual aspect of this musical form. Disregard for or indifference to everything that is visual in it is so far-reaching that many histories of opera have been written without so much as mentioning the history of ballet in opera, which is erroneously - not only by dancers - regarded as part of the visual component of opera, with ballet itself regarded wrongly as a purely visual art in general. After that nothing is left to be said about the omission of scenic history from the standard descriptions of the genesis and development of operatic form.

It is beyond dispute that of all the components, music remains the focal point of every operatic work. This is true even of Wagner's works, in which he sought to unite music with various arts such as drama, poetry, painting, sculpture and architecture. The most compelling argument for disregarding all the nonmusical elements in the opera is the viability of operatic music and symphonic ballet. They are capable of sustaining independent life on gramophone records and in concert halls, but all the other elements that go into opera and ballet are not, apart from the dancing itself which in some cases can exist without music. To rectify this view it should be added right away that most composers did not intend their operas only for the phonograph record, nor their ballets only for the concert hall. Instead, in the process of creation. they visualized their work in its entirety, in time and space.

DR. NADEZDA MOSUSOVA teaches at the Institute of Musicology in Belgrade, Yugoslavia.

Therefore we are bewildered by the fact that in the opinion of many musicians, the visual aspect of operatic art is concerned with such unimportant things as stage movement, filling the stage with scenery and dressing the singers. Generally, music historians leave such technicalities to theatre and art chroniclers in the belief that that is no business of theirs. The latter again, lacking professional training in music, more often than not confine themselves to the problems of scenic design and the architecture of musical theatre.

If they happen to take account of the operatic components other than music, musicologists will consider in what way a score is reflected on the scene and design or how the latter is adapted to the music and the plot. It has almost become a cliche to acknowledge that music influences the *mise-en-scène,* i.e. that design and costumes fit in with the music (or rather with the plot on which it is based), even without getting into a serious discussion of *Gesamtkunstwerk.* Thus the esthetic question of the interaction of music, acting, scenery and costumes quite often remains unanalyzed, in spite of the fact that the visual side of an operatic production does not primarily involve the technical, material side (which many operatic listeners and champions of the so-called absolute music regard as an unimportant element in the opera), but rather the internal visual concept of the music/drama as it is dictated by the music itself.

Much still remains to be said about the visual aspect of operatic music, not only as regards directing (throoughly worked out by Felsenstein), but also the design and costumes. The idea that scenery is influenced by music is taken for granted. But *how* does music, or rather music/drama, influence the development of stage design in general or the creation of a given stage or lighting design - this has hardly been explained. Can, for instance, a single composer influence the development of stage decoration? It is these questions that must be answered as we come to the point: *can stage design have an influence on music/drama?*

Can stage design in general influence the development of music/drama or indirectly inspire a music/drama to be composed? The answer could be yes, it can - provided the stage setting is, or becomes, an independent work of art. The idea that decor can be treated as a work of art per se, not only to be displayed in a museum but to be used on the stage, was made material when famous Russian easel painters, invited in the last century to bring high expression to opera and ballet productions as a whole, entered the world of musical stage. Among the most outstanding results of their work were brilliant settings by Benois, Bakst and Roerich, devised for Diaghilev's Saisons des Ballets Russes in Paris.

In Russia, the curtain and scene-with-backcloth became a picture worth admiring for its own sake. Audiences of the *Belle Epoque* went to the performances at St. Petersburg and Moscow theatres not only to hear the music and watch the dancing, but also to allow the beautiful scenery made by Korovin, Golovin and other significant easel masters, to capture their imagination. Such romantic, art-for-art's sake attitude towards design and designers still prevails, especially in ballet. In the history of stage design and musical scene, this appears to be the period when painter-artists took over the job from artisan-designers. The beauty they created was not quite surpassed by those who succeeded them, Appia, Craig and Boll, the designers to whom we are indebted for establishing the scenic design as a branch of art in its own right.

It is possible for an opera of ballet to be inspired by an independent work of art, such as a picture or a sculpture, as well as by the style of a historical epoch, a given milieu (especially in ballet) in much the same way as the so-called program music is inspired by literary works and paintings. Since both opera and ballet are partly programmatic, such assumptions do not seem unreasonable at all. This finally brings us to the question whether it is conceivable for a music/drama or ballet to be devised for a specific type of scenic setting or a particular kind of costume - and we find that the answer is affirmative - this has already been done in practice.

Would it be possible for decor to have an influence on drama as well? Could we approach the history of the drama/theatre from the standpoint of stage design being used as a creative impulse for the playwright? Certainly not, because decoration in the drama/theatre is in no case regarded as an independent work of art. It aims to be purely functional, always made to suit the plot and the acting.

On the other hand, decoration in musical theatre is not made to support the singers-actors. Having served in its heyday as a means of expression, not of function, the stage setting in music/drama and ballet was conceived not only as an environment for the singing and dancing, but as the equal of music, or both music and choreography. Think of Roerich's scenery for Wagner's music/dramas (as performed in Moscow in 1912) or the settings for the ballets *Prince Igor* or the *Rite of Spring* made by the same painter for the Ballets Russes. That was the moment when the stage setting, together with opera and ballet costume (especially the latter) was promoted to a work of art and the sung/danced theatre was definitely separated from the spoken theatre on the visual level. It became perfectly clear that the same decor just wouldn't do for *Othello* performed as drama, opera or ballet, even if all three of them are based on Shakespeare's play.

Many of the symbolist painters, like Roerich, Sapunov, Somov or

Sudejkin, worked for the theatre, contributing to that field real works of art, too. But such independence was bound to result in a discrepancy between the design and the drama because their works became the predominant feature on the stage. We can be sure that the stage sketches for Ibsen's plays made by Edvard Munch, surpassed some of the dramatic and poetic thoughts of the playwright (in the same way as the dramatic character of Wagner's music often greatly surpasses the dramatic features of his plots). Reinhardt was hardly aware that the famous painter had interfered with his all-for-the actor principle - a standpoint unchanging in spite of all the possible metamorphoses of scenic image.

Let us return to the question of how the music is reflected on the stage setting. The direct influence is not so easy to depict as it may seem at first sight. Paradoxically, it is sometimes harder than in the reverse case. It is clear that the decor comes to its highest expression when inspired by the power of music. Only when united with music can the setting, with all the richness of its colours, create the highly condensed emotional world on the stage.

It should be remembered, however, that stage setting does not have equal importance for every kind of music/drama or symphonic ballet. Each one of them is single in its kind in the sense that each opera or ballet has its own, unique musical form carrying specific requirements as regards its scenic realization. There are music/dramas which are almost indifferent to the stage setting aspect and there are ballets which can be performed without any scenery. In spite of this, for psychological reasons which are synesthetic in character, the linkage is tighter between painting and music and more loose between painting and drama and acting. The vision of a truly colorful - and therefore provocative - stage setting, can inspire a composer of opera and ballet, far more than a playwright. Stravinsky was a musical genius, but could it not be that the mere thought of having Benois or Roerich by his side inspired him to do what he has done?

Speaking in this way of the decor only, we are doing injustice to the costume, which is very important for the music/drama and even more for ballet. It is important in the spoken theatre too because, sometimes, the image of a role can emerge from a costume-sketch, just as from a portrait. But as we know, the realization of garments and make-up comes at the end of preparing a play, the first emphasis being placed on creating the role. In opera, and especially in ballet, it is of vital importance for the costume to suit not only the singer and dancer, but also the character of music. What to say about the ballet costumes designed by Bakst! Even lesser celebrities were able to prompt composers. Take the case of the full-evening ballet *The Sleeping Beauty* composed by

Stravinsky's famous predecessor Peter Tchaikovsky. The director of the Imperial Theatres in St. Petersburg, Vassily Vseveložsky, a skillful costume designer himself, wanted to make a ballet scenario based on the fairy-tales by Charles Perrault. "I shall produce the *mise-en-scène* in the style of Louis XIV" - he wrote to Tchaikovsky, urging him to write music for it. The composer fulfilled Vsevoložsky's wish bringing into the work not only his romantic style but introducing some classical and even baroque patterns suited to the *sujet* and the proposed scenary.

The development of decor, however, was not only due to music/drama but also to the evolution of all arts in the latter part of the nineteenth century. The crucial factor was technical evolution, especially the introduction of electric lighting. Richard Wagner, the creator of music/drama as a genre did not play a decisive role in the development of decor, but he was well aware that scenery and its colours have an important function in creating the proper mood. With him started the interest in engaging easel painters for the opera stage. It is known that Wagner wanted Arnold Bocklin for his "Ring" cycle and engaged Paul Joukowsky for *Parsifal.* He had a direct influence on contemporary painters and contributed to arousing the interest of Russian easel painters in music and the interest of musicians in painting. Owing to Wagner's art, the painters began to "illustrate" music in the opera, which until then had been regarded unworthy of a true artist. In Russia, Nikolai Roerich, the pioneer of the Russian symbolism and central figure of the *World of Art* and Nikolai Rimski-Korsakov, the thirty-years-older member of the "Mighty Five," spent their time studying the interralationship between colors in music and painting.

Apart from being talented ethnographers and historians, easel-painters scenographers had literary gifts too, and wrote ballet scenarios, like Vsevoložsky. Roerich applied both his artistic talent and his literary abilities in producing the *sujet* for Stravinsky's *Rite of Spring.* Leon Bakst devised scenery and costumes and wrote the scenarios for the Rimski-Korsakov's ballet *Scheherzade* (whose plot differs from that of the author's) and *Istar* (music by Vincent d'Indy). Benois accomplished various tasks in the production of *Pavillon d'Armide* (music by Nikolai Tcerepnin) as well as in Stravinsky's *Petrushka,* which is the model of the *Gesamtkunstwerk, par-excellence.*

In spite of various experiments performed after World War I, the influence of the art of painting on opera and ballet decor was kept alive between two wars owing to numerous capable stage artists, adherents of the Russian pre-revolutionary scenographic school who joined European theatres in the wake of the Russian revolution. A good many of them, including a fairly large number of operatic artists, ballet dancers and choreographers, settled in Yugoslavia. This had a stimulating effect on Yugoslav opera and ballet composers who began to write for the music stage; however, they were frustrated by the cultural life dominated by the spoken drama and its directors.

Due to occasional penetration of theatrical directors and scenographers into opera houses, which is at the present time an accepted practice everywhere, decor has come to be treated once again as a functional element rather than as a means of expression. In some cases opera was consciously identified with drama or brought up-to-date through modernization of the plot. This attitude led to the most recent and, in the opinion of many admirers of Wagner's art, shocking production of *The Ring of the Nibelung* at Bayreuth. The influence of "all-for-the-actor" decoration can still be seen both in motion-picture and televised operatic productions.

The emergence of television gave an impetus to many composers all over the world as well as in Yugoslavia to create for the new medium. Directors and designers were offered new possibilities, new approaches and interesting solutions. In our country the composers have shown a distinct interest in a special type of musical theatre, the psychological music monodrama (e.g. the *Diary of a Madman* after Gogol's tale, composed by the Serbian author Stanojlo Rajičić) in which the functional treatment of decor and costume could find a justification. find a justification.

Some of the contemporary experiments in the field of directing and stage setting on television brought together again here and there modern stage designers and easel painters of the past. We will cite here the well-known production of *Carmen,* telecast from the Vienna opera in December 1978, in which the scenery was obviously based on the motifs and colors of the Spanish paintings.

In conclusion, here is an example of the direct transfer of the shapes of the drawings and mood of the colors from the canvas to the decor and costumes and then to the scenario, music and choreography, carried out in a recent Hungarian television production of a ballet. The motifs of the Hungarian painter Tivadar Csontváry were reproduced in decor and costumes and then given to the composer Frigyes Hidas to invent the plot and music. This televised production of the ballet *Cedar,* realized in homage to the Hungarian symbolist painter, represents an unusually successful experiment illustrating the direct influence of decor on music, which might be realized in other media too.

MODELS OF SCENERY AND COSTUMES IN THE PERFORMING ARTS DEPARTMENT OF THE BIBLIOTHEQUE NATIONALE, PARIS

by Cecile Giteau

Many fundamental matters concerning scenery models have already been discussed during the first working sessions by previous speakers, in particular by Howard Bay in his general introduction to the theme of this Congress and by Anthony Ibbotson, who dealt specifically with the techniques of execution and the conditions for preservation.

To avoid unnecessary repetition, I shall present here a less complete paper than the one listed in the summary you are holding and shall call to mind and pinpoint the fundamental principles governing the growth of the models collection of the Performing Arts Department of the Bibliotheque Nationale and how they are catalogued for use in research.

First of all, I shall briefly describe the characteristics of our collections:

a. around 25,000 models or plates of scenery and costumes are kept in the collections of the Performing Arts Department of the Bibliotheque Nationale. Most of them date to the 20th century, from its beginning to modern times; only around a hundred predate 1900.

b. the original collections and subsequent additions come from various sources; acquisitions are usually made after a production.

c. original models are acquired, or borrowed from stage designers and theaters to be photographed by the photographic service of the Bibliotheque Nationale: since 1939, color transparencies have been made of 16,000 models (at least three shots are taken: one for the back-up files, one for

---

CECILE GITEAU is the Director of the Department of Performing Arts at the Biblioteque Nationale in Paris.

circulation and one for the potential file of duplicates).

The diverse origins of the models that we acquire make identification and cataloguing difficult. Models are donated under a bequest, or purchased, either singly or in sets. They are sent to us directly by professionals in the theater (stage designers, producers or directors of theaters or companies) by their heirs or by collectors. They may be acquired from specialized or general dealers (the specialized dealers are often collectors themselves). They may also be acquired at auctions, for the Bibliotheque Nationale is permitted to exercise a right of preemption.

This list looks simple; but in practice, many problems of awareness arise in the choice of these documents. Let us say that we wish to safeguard the largest possible number of models which are of documentary interest or represent an artistic heritage; their preservation has been ignored for too long.

Apart from budgetary problems, which are often negatively determinant, certain principles dictate our line of conduct, or policy of acquisitions. The following, in brief, are the initial aspects determining our choices: the authenticity of the model as a representation of the performance; the model's artistic quality, its degree of inventiveness or originality· the model's importance to the complete performance, its development, its tonality of expression; the maker of the model; the importance of the performance in the history of the theater (important production, creation of a piece); the written notation concerning the technical execution; and the follow-ups or sets (essential elements to a deeper knowledge of the performance).

These more or less subjective or relative parameters are not always easy to articulate. Whenever possible, it is preferable to check the information from stage designers themselves if their memory is sufficiently accurate. The models and dramatic texts have variants, subsequent versions or adaptations. Is this a model of the first performance, of a repeat performance or a tour? (example: Jean-Denis Malcles). Was the scenery changed during the lifetime of a show because of a change in the site of the performance? (example: the TNP at the Festival of Avignon and in the Theatre of the Chaillot Palace).

Does this model represent preparatory studies, or a project which was not completed? Was this performance really given, or is this model just a fantasy of scenery, with all the appearances of a finished model? The typical case of Gordon Craig has frequently been mentioned in this context.

Is this really the original model? Painters are sometimes tempted to improve the quality of the model after the performance, or even to repeat one of their great successes in a painting; the many versions of the scenery for ***Petrushka*** by Benois may be cited as example. I have even seen a well-known painter reproduce a model from memory more than thirty years later and not hesitate to put the original date under his signature!

Is this a training exercise? Two stage designers, Paul Colin and Yves Bonnat, whose extensive teaching activities paralleled their own careers, made training models for demonstrations. Furthermore, it is evident that there were sometimes two analogous or very similar series of models: one for the workshop and the other for the stage designer or producer (examples, *Electre* by Giraudoux staged by Louis Jouvet with models by Bouchene; *Les Caprices de Marianne* staged by Gaston Baty with scenery by Emile Bertin).

The problems of identification are greatly minimized if the work has been left in its group and the models are filed together (written production, technical documents, photographs of scenes, etc.). Among the main bequests given to our Department in this manner, we must mention the collections of Gordon Craig, Jacques Copeau, Louis Jouvet, Gaston Baty, Georges Pitoeff. Larger sets in a certain unit have also been sent to us by stage designers or their heirs, including Walter Rene Fuerst, Wladimir Jedrinsky, Jean Hugo, Robert and Sonia Delaunay, Lucien Coutaud.

Once the models are dispersed, the problems which arise are sometimes insoluble: identification becomes more difficult because the documents are usually scattered by people who lack the most elementary knowledge of the theatre or who, for whatever reason, are interested in concealing the true origin of the document. We have spent these last few months, for instance, trying to rediscover the models, unfortunately scattered, of a great Parisian theatre whose other artistic files had been sent to us: this tracking work is not yet finished, but the end is in sight! Another, all too frequent example of dismemberment is a public auction, prepared in haste by official appraisers who, for business purposes, reconstitute imaginary lots each containing a "bait" without the least respect for the unity of the dramatic work. Sometimes the price charged for a model places us in a difficult position: the choice of an act, a scene or an actor is often harrowing, particularly if an authorization to photograph the other models cannot be expected.

In view of these difficulties in identification, we thought it wiser and more effective to prepare the models for scientific use by working in successive steps, using a rigorous, uniform basic method, except for large collections for which a descriptive catalog can be made. Our working method is as follows: We follow the general cataloguing principles of the CREDAS code, mentioned repeatedly at this Congress, as its main purpose is to enable us to list references to the documents on the card identifying a performance. Photographing the documents is essential: preferably one color transparency and one black and white print. For material reasons, we have not yet been able to do this work as systematically as would be desirable. Temporary forms are made out which can be taken up again, completed or corrected. The columns on them are as follows (see enclosure). Correct identification of the documents requires the use of various types of documentation: photographs of scenes, programs, press releases, etc.

This work proceeds in stages, enabling us to draw up progressively a methodical and well founded inventory.

Our aim is to draw up a complete, even if summary, list of models in France dating from 1930 to our own day. This work was begun with the aid of temporary collaborators whose mobility, while at times a handicap, has been a beneficial constraint for us. Under difficult conditions, we have already obtained encouraging results: we have been able to find unknown works, fill in gaps and proceed with acquisitions.

Our conclusions as to the scientific usefulness of such models are optimistic but guarded, for several reasons: it is rare that a model, even if it appears on the whole to be a true representation of the performance, is strictly identical with the actual scenery; a two-dimensional plate is an imperfect document for it is the conversion of a three-dimensional sphere to two dimensions; the original artistic temperament of the stage designer is reflected in the model, regardless of the person who made it.

For example: the very personal style of Christian Berard or of Jean Denis Malcles creates atmosphere; even on a mere backgroundcurtain, the very rigorous shapes of Felix Labisse call to mind practical scenery perspectives; and the very poetic and naive style used by Jacques Noel for the works of Ionesco is of such intensity that it attains the surreal.

The model, after all, does not do justice to the diversity of the creative process in its variety and complexity.

Too few in-depth studies have been made: the same works are generally reproduced or cited. In fact, the models are important testimonials to the development of the conception and organization of theatrical work, but this can be seen only from a certain perspective and from a good number of documents.

Furthermore, in exhibits with a theatrical theme it is undeniable that models, which recall a moment of the performance, are an eye-catching visual element and sensitize the visitor to the problems of the theatre.

The problem remains unsolved: models, an eternal compromise between artistic, pictorial and documentary value.

ELEMENTS OF A METHOD FOR USING MODELS OF SCENERY OR OF SCENERY ARRANGEMENTS AS STUDY DOCUMENTS

by André Veinstein

Three-dimensional models occupy a privileged position among the many types of documents and objectives of documentary interest available for the practice and study of the theatre, most particularly documents and objects made during the preparation of or reconstruction of a performance.

They are of interest for theatre practice (construction, information), theoretical study (history, esthetics, etc.), research (theory, and/or practice) and training of practitioners or theoreticians. Models can be used for discussing the following subjects: scenery (traditional painted cloth of the Italian style theatre), arrangement (play area built), the architecture of the place of the performance and the machinery, lighting and sound devices, furniture, accessories, etc.

In spite of the difficult problems of conservation, an ever-growing number of models are housed in libraries, museums or documentation centers. They must be distinguished with a view to their characteristic differences in order to find their different documentary value. One type of model, far from the least numerous, is made for research and experimentation with a view to practice, study or instruction. Such models frequently mark a stage in the work or a step in instruction. They have the value of documenting a step, a stage. They are instruments of provisional work, the concrete expression of an idea. They are of double interest: a specific state and a specific stage.

A second type is a so-called working model. During preparations for a performance, different models are made to see how they work. They reflect the various stages, often fragmentary and usually provisional; some of these models may seem to reflect the final stage, with all the annoying consequences such a mistake may bring.

A third category of models is that used for the actual performance,

---

ANDRE VEINSTEIN, of the University of Paris, serves as Editor of *Performing Arts Libraries and Museums of the World.*

during the construction of the scenery. A fourth category of models consists of those built after the performance and thus reconstructs all the elements of the scenery or arrangement. In other words, there are experimental, working, final and reconstructed models.

The documentary interest of these four types of models usually lies in the base data of the scenery, scene craft (in all its aspects), the stage setting and the play. More specifically, they will show the configuration and the profile of the play area(s), the installation of the scenery, the decorative motifs, the movable elements and the machinery for same, accessories, furniture. Shapes, measurable dimensions, colors, lighting, movement: such are the most specific data which can be gathered from the best models in the last two categories. When there are only working models, they must not be disregarded for reasons we shall indicate below.

Strict methodological precautions must be taken, which we shall briefly indicate below. The first precaution is to collect all the information concerning the architecture of the site of the performance (drawings, dimensions) and to evaluate the model's accuracy as to measurements and shapes of the scenery or arrangement on the basis of what is known of the site. The second precaution is to identify the category of model being used: is it a final model, or a reconstructed, a working or an experimental model?

It is therefore essential to use all supplementary or comparative information available: building plans, two-dimensional models and sketches, written stage directions, photos, written or oral eye-witness accounts, etc. But if the model is identified as a reconstruction, it is advisable to check on any changes which might have been made after the model was built, for instance in the dimensions, colors, installation of scenery. If there is neither a final nor a reconstructed model, but only one or more working models, it is advisable to use the data from them, for they may contain very valuable information, but, of course, the precautions regarding final models must be strictly observed.

On the basis of the foregoing, an outline may be proposed of the method which may be used for the various types of models, as follows:

I. *Appearance of the Model*

- dimensions, scale. Over-all dimensions; dimensions of the various elements
- materials used
- color
- movable or stationary elements
- lighting equipment
- sound equipment

II. *Origin of the Model*
- title of the work in question
- author of the work
- producer
- choreographer
- composer
- scenographer
- decorator
- costume designer
- lighting designer
- engineers
- others
- date of the premiere for which the model was made
- name of the site, of the theatre and of the company
- date of the first performance for which the model was made
- name of the builder of the model

III. *Date the Model was Made*

IV. *Original Reasons for Making and Using the Model*
- putting on a performance
- research; experimentation
- study
- instruction
- repeat performance
- cultural diffusion
- reconstruction

V. *Description of the Model*
- Subjects:
- scenery (or elements of scenery)
- arrangement (or elements of arrangement)
- architecture
- machinery
- equipment (light, sound)
- accessories
- furniture
- other

VI. *Use of Supplementary Documents* (for identifying the model, categorizing it, analyzing it and for its critical evaluation).
- preparatory sketches
- two-dimensional models
- working models
- installation of scenery
- conduct

- written stage directions
- drawing of the hall or place of performance
- photos of the scenery and/or of the arrangement(s)
- photos of scenes
- layouts for the lighting devices
- layouts for the sound devices
- documentary films
- videotapes
- written or oral eye witness accounts
- others

IX. Set design for an Ionic Temple, inventory number DTM 206/1975 A-Q, the Drottningholm Theatre Museum.

X. Side wing (stage right nearest to the proscenium) from above Ionic Temple set.

XI. Side wing (stage right) from above Ionic Temple set.

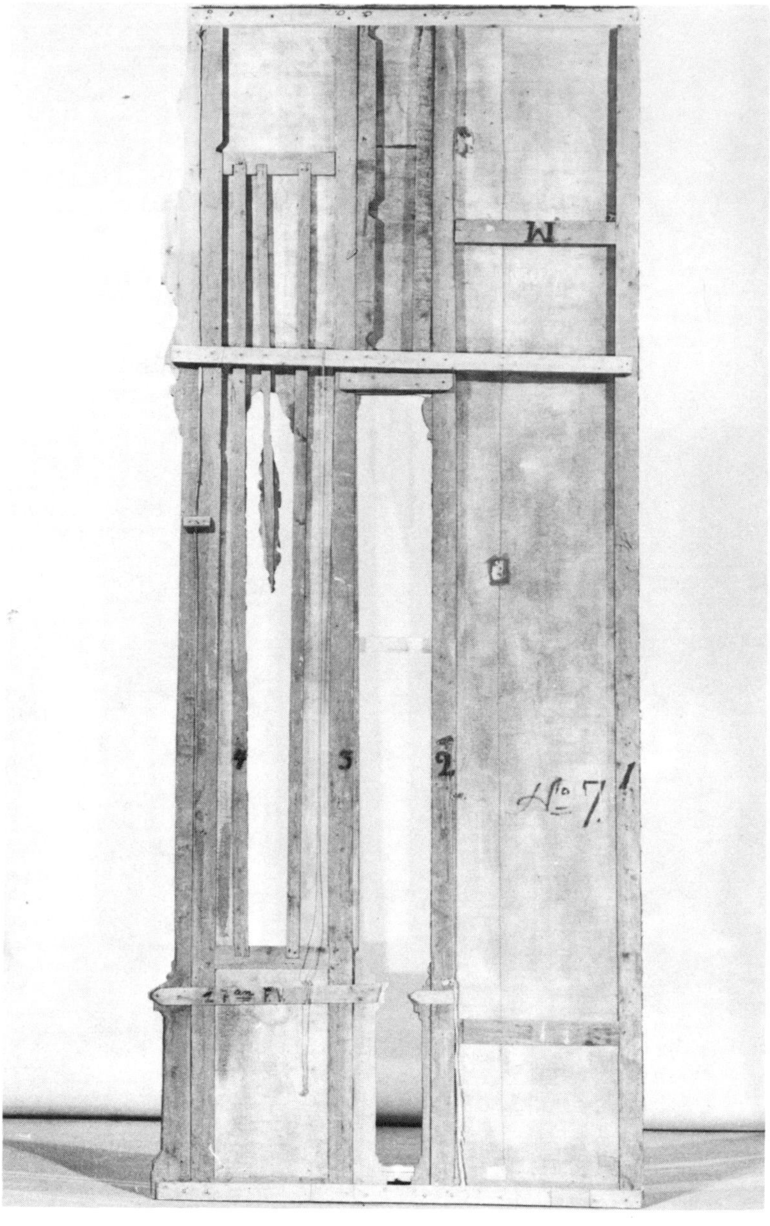

XII. Side wing (stage right) from above Ionic Temple set, photo graphed from behind.

XIII. Center wing (center stage right) from above Ionic Temple set.

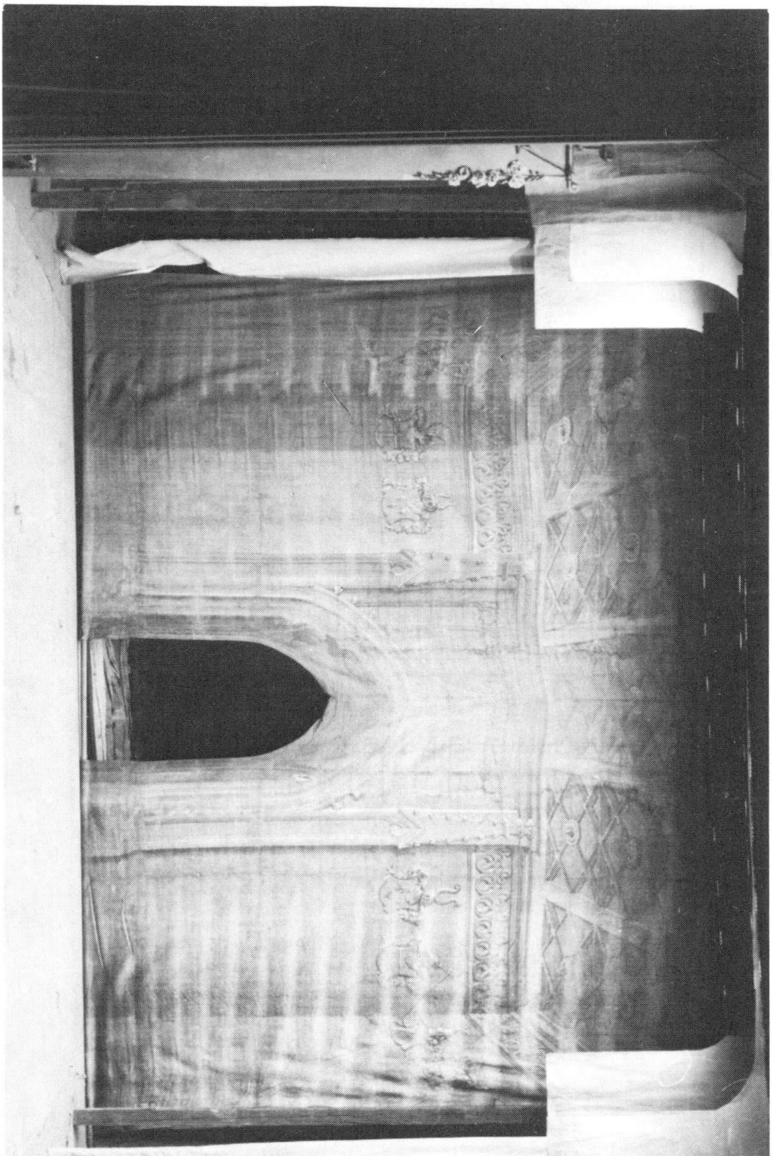

XIV. Back drop for a Gothic hall setting, Ludwigsburg Court Theatre.

XV. Back drop and stage left lateral wings from Classicist chamber setting, Ludwigsburg Court Theatre.

XVI. Back drop for Rural interior setting with staircase, Ludwigsburg Court Theatre.

XVII. Back drop for Forest setting, Ludwigsburg Court Theatre.

XVIII. Complete setting with back drop and four pair of wings, for "Sala del grotto," Ludwigsburg Court Theatre.

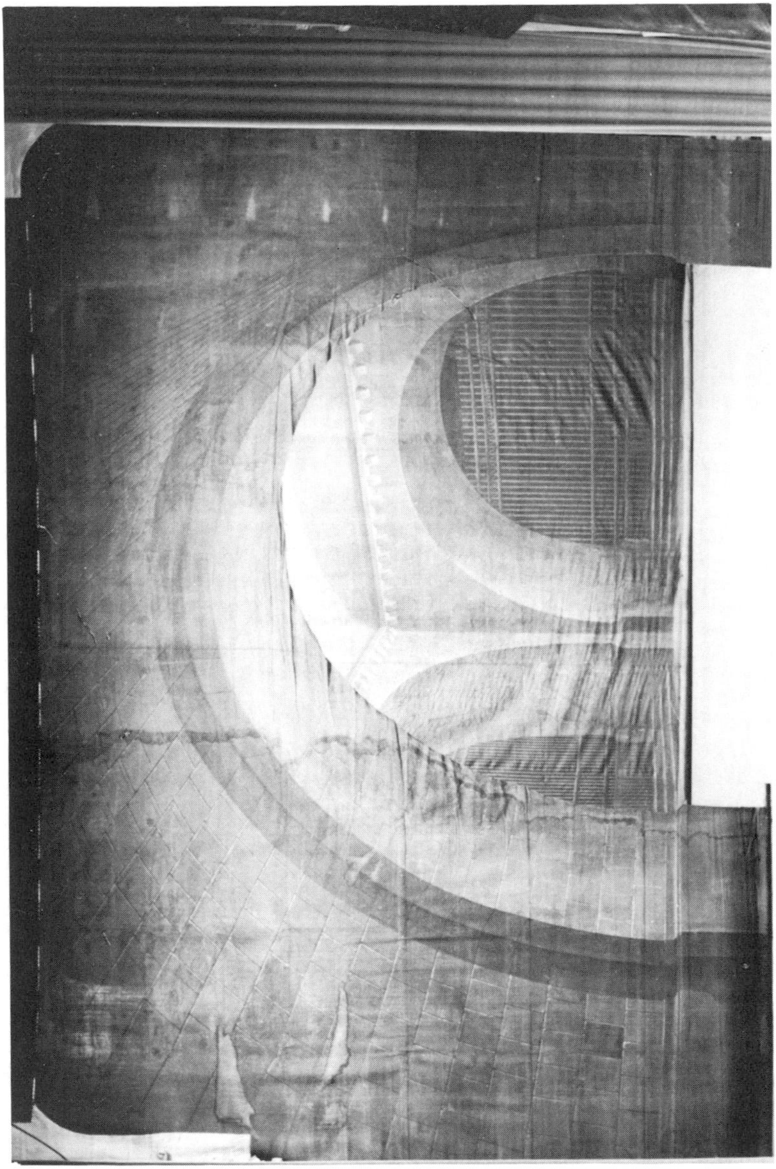

XIX. Cut cloth drop and back drop for Prison scene, Ludwigsburg Court Theatre.

XX. Stage design by Christian Friedrich Beuther (1777-1856) of Prison scene, for comparison to Illus. XIX, Theatermuseum, Universitat, Köln.

XXI. Back drop for Peasant's chamber with stove, Ludwigsburg Court Theatre.

XXII. Stage design by Christian Friedrich Beuther of Peasant's chamber with stove, for comparison to Illus. XXI, Theatermuseum, Universitat, Köln.

XXIII. Backdrop for vaulted alcove with classicist drapery, showing damage to lower stage right corner, Ludwigsburg Court Theatre.

XXIV. Back drop for Classicist hall setting, showing heavy damage to fabric, Ludwigsburg Court Theatre.

AUDIO-VISUAL TECHNIQUES USED IN EXHIBITS: VARIOUS PROCEDURES

by Marie Françoise Christout

In view of the increasingly important role played by the audio-visual media during the last ten years, it is now impossible to avoid their use in organizing an exhibition. In this connection, I must point out that the various visits we have made in New York during this Congress have enabled us to appreciate the excellent manner in which our American friends, particularly Dr. Mary C. Henderson, have used these audio-visual techniques.

Audio-visual installations to supplement the presentation of the works of art are used by almost all large exhibitions today, particularly those dealing with art history, i.e. retrospective shows of one artist such as Courbet, Chardin or Gainsborough, those dealing with a whole school, or those covering a period seen from a specific point of view. But this method is practically a must in the field of the performing arts, which are essentially visual and auditory. It is indispensable for the film and the dance, the arts of motion.

But its use poses various theoretical and practical problems which must be considered before the choice is made. The choice of processes to be used depends on various factors.

The first aspect to consider is the requirements of the subject; an exhibition may be dedicated to a playwright such as Moliere, Shakespeare, Brecht, Evreinoff, O'Neill or Giraudoux; in this case, the literary work and its interpretations must be emphasized and the latter sometimes compared to each other. In effect, over the years, the public's taste and the techniques for staging a play have changed.

An exhibition may be dedicated to a personality in the world of the theatre: a stage designer, a producer, a choreographer, a decorator, such as Jacques Copeau, Edward Gordon Craig, Andre Barsacq, Jean Villar, Jouvet, Jean Renoir, Auguste Bournonville; in such a case, the originality of the stage design, the film or the choreography should be

---

MARIE FRANCOISE CHRISTOUT is with the Department of Performing Arts of the Biblioteque Nationale in Paris.

demonstrated. For an actor, a singer or dancer such as Sarah Bernhardt, Eleanora Duse, Fedor Chaliapin, Anna Pavlova, Serge Lifar, Christian Berard, it is important to illustrate the personality of the interpreter through his main roles.

An exhibit may also honor a specific company, such as the tercentenary of the Comedie Française, the bicentennial of the Bolshoi of Moscow, the fiftieth anniversary of the ballet troupes of Serge Diaghilev, or Rolf de Mare. Then it must show the repertory as well as the company and pay special attention to its most famous members: Talma, Rachel or Nijinsky.

Finally, an exhibition may be mounted on an art form such as the circus, fireworks, movie houses or ballet from a national or international viewpoint.

Each type of subject requires individual preparation and must be looked at from a different viewpoint. Naturally, the organizer must keep in mind which elements he has on hand and can use, and which he must acquire or perhaps make for each exhibit. Obviously, this depends on the often scarce financial means at his disposal. In effect, he can rarely proceed freely on the basis of his choice and use the processes which would fit each case; only commercial exhibits supported by patrons are entirely free to employ whatever method best fits the exhibit. Liberal collaboration between cultural organizations and large companies such as Kodak, Thompson, IBM, etc., sometimes permits greater use of the available technical means to enhance exhibits on the performing arts. In France, the national museums have not hesitated to have recourse to this type of participation. All cultural organizations could be encouraged to use this procedure to their advantage.

We shall review the principal processes now in use, starting with the simplest, and the advantages and drawbacks of each. It is understood that this list is not complete and that new techniques with new formulas are constantly being perfected. Three main procedures can be distinguished: 1) aural 2) visual 3) audio-visual.

First of all, we shall discuss *sound* for the exhibit, which may be produced by two methods, sometimes used jointly:

By pinpoint sound, with the aid of a listening device with one or preferably two earphones. This device must be placed in the margin of the walkway, so that one or two visitors may stop without disturbing the circulation of the rest. It uses an audio tape lasting some twenty minutes at most, usually composed of several supplementary fragments. To avoid stopping the listener too long while yet bringing him a greater knowledge of the various aspects of the play and of the stage business, one can in this way juxtapose tapes of the author or producer with extracts from the plays, each one chosen so as to clearly characterize a specific aspect of the work, or a moment in it, or from the repertory of a company, such as the Comedie Francaise, using its most famous members. While brief - from one or two to 4-5 minutes - each extract must be easily understood and, as far as possible, interpreted by artists of unquestioned talent under optimal recording conditions available when it was made. It is obvious that the listener must be told of the date of the recording if it is defective; for instance, the recording of the voice of Jean Giraudoux (around 1939) has had to be speeded up in order to eliminate some surface noise. This is even more true of the voices of famous actors prior to the twentieth century, such as Sarah Bernhardt or Monnet-Sully. The extracts should be separated by brief musical interludes and the listener must be able to see the contents of the tape on a label so that he may switch the tape on or off as he wishes. Here too the rarity and the defects in each recorded extract must be mentioned.

Background music for the exhibit may also be provided. It is essential to avoid spoken text on such a tape, for the repetition quickly becomes irksome to the visitor. On the other hand, a deft use of extracts of background music easily puts the visitor into the proper mood for the exhibit, whether it pertains to the East, to classical or to modern works. But silent intervals are essential, so as not to saturate the public's attention, but keep it alert. It is understood that the music must be carefully selected to allow for each transition between different works and to avoid too much contrast on the sound tape between high and low notes.

We turn now to another process using visual elements to supplement the documents on exhibit: an automatic slide show for the visitors. This process enables the public to view many documents and to gather supplementary information on the period, on the conditions of the performance, or on the scenic techniques used. It may be in the form of simple continuous projections without sound. Or, with specialized techniques, sound and synchronized comments can be added; but this is at present a difficult process and requires great care in recording the sound. Finally, if adequate financial means are available and an organization which specializes in this type of installation can be used, more complex processes may be employed including linked dissolves and the enlargement of certain details. In the latter case, close collaboration is essential with the personnel in charge of coordinating the various operations: installation, sound and work on the documents; they must be experts chosen by the organizers of the exhibit.

The organizer of an exhibit may use a magnetoscope either to project films on the subject of the exhibit, or documents if they are movie films or TV films and broadcasts. Here again the choice is difficult: one must keep in mind the artistic and educational quality of the film or the broadcast, its duration, which may not be too long, and the nature of the documents it uses. For instance, for the tercentenary exhibit of the Comedie Française at the Biblioteque Nationale, we discarded all the broadcasts based on title stills made from original documents on exhibit.

On the other hand, this type of projection may supplement an exhibit and bring it to life, enabling the visitor to assimilate a type of information which he might not understand without this aid, in particular of the historical background, the atmosphere, the climate at the time of the performance. In 1980, we conducted a very interesting experiment at the Bibliotheque Nationale in collaboration with the National Institute of Audiovisual Aid and the Comedie Française. But at that time, the problem of the actors' rights was more simple.

It is obvious that the use of these different processes poses problems of space, of selection, of execution; sometimes the aid of experienced professional technicians is needed to solve these problems. Once in place, these devices must be carefully supervised and maintained. They must be protected from any handling other than for service. The financial aspect must not be neglected in drawing up an estimate for an exhibit.

As is shown every day by examples from all over the world, audio-visual techniques will be increasingly necessary in the future in any large exhibit on the performing arts.

EIGHTEENTH-CENTURY STAGE SETTINGS AT THE COURT THEATRES OF DROTTNINGHOLM AND GRIPSHOLM

by Barbro Stribolt

My address will concern itself with two of the three eighteenth century Swedish court theatres which still remain in a reasonable state of preservation: namely, that belonging to the Palace of Drottningholm just outside Stockholm, and that in Gripsholm Castle, about thirty miles inland from the capital. These theatres, together with that at the Palace of Rosersberg, possess unique collections of stage sets from the eighteenth and early nineteenth centuries. The dramatic art they represent is bound by close ties to European traditions, and so they are of unique value to historical research, not only in Sweden but also in a much wider context.

When the Drottningholm Theatre was put in order in 1921, sets were found in basement, attic, and anterooms as well as on the stage itself. However, we cannot claim that these sets have no counterparts elsewhere, as we can for the stage machinery. There are a few complete collections of eighteenth-century sets, with their side-wings and backdrops, still in existence at various places in Czechoslovakia, and the remnants of sets from the same period are found sporadically elsewhere. The richest of these rested in storerooms belonging to the eighteenth-century theatre in Ludwigsburg (Württemberg), in West Germany.

As regards stage design, there are half-a-dozen complete sets in typical Bibiena style still reposing in Krumlov Castle, Schwartzenberg, in southern Czechoslovakia. They were made by stage designers Johann Wetschel and Leo Merkel, all, apparently, in 1766, when the theatre was fitted out. (This also happens to be the year from which we date the present Drottningholm Theatre.) The well-preserved stage sets belonging to the small court theatre of Litomisl in northern Czechoslovakia are of considerably later date–from the 1790s. In addi-

---

BARBRO STRIBOLT is the Curator of the Drottningholm Theatre Museum in Sweden.

tion to the artistic value of the Litomisl sets, they are interesting in that the original sketches, made by Joseph Platzer, have been preserved.

None of the collections I have mentioned so far can compare favorably with the sets now stored at Drottningholm, however. In addition to these, Sweden also possesses eight complete and extraordinarily well-preserved stage decors from the period 1782 to 1785 in the Court Theatre at Gripsholm Castle. Other sets now preserved at Drottningholm come from the Court Theatre at Rosersberg, where performances were held during the first decades of the nineteenth century. By no means the least valuable thing about this Swedish collection of stage sets from the period 1766 to the first decades of the 1800s is that it allows us to follow at first-hand the changes in style which occurred during those years. The period was one of transition not only in the history of stage decor but also in the whole manner of creating and experiencing the theatre as an art form.

The Drottningholm collection of original eighteenth-century sets was first presented to a wider public with the appearance in 1937 of the book on the Court Theatres of Drottningholm and Gripsholm by late Professor Agne Beijer. This fine pioneering work on the subject appeared in a limited edition of only a few hundred copies and has long since been out of print. The various items were brought together and photographed as individual stage settings. In this way, the unique collection became known to a wider circle of specialists.

Nonetheless, Beijer's book is not definitive, and complete scientific arrangement of the collection still remains to be done. Since 1975, broad cataloguing and inventory work has been pursued steadily at the Drottningholm Theatre Museum. The detailed cataloguing of the sets is of prime importance because of their uniqueness and because they provide us with such complete evidence of the scenographic situation at the end of the eighteenth century.

Every single object has now been carefully photographed and described. A great deal of the information we have gathered has come directly from the objects themselves, while other scraps of knowledge have been gleaned from old extant inventories. Then we have recorded such details as fastenings, fragments of rope, various kinds of repairs, and so on—all of them small things in themselves but, taken as a whole and used for comparison, they can contribute importantly to the reconstruction of a process of development.

Among the old inventories relating to the sets is one which is very detailed and of much interest. It was drawn up by what translates as the Royal Theatrical Directorate in Stockholm in 1808 under the heading: "Sets, of Which the Greater Share Are Said To Have Been Used at Drottningholm, Where Some of Which Are Stored, Others in the Set

Repository in the City" (that is, Stockholm). This inventory shows that it was not unusual for sets to be moved among the various court theatres and the Royal Opera House in Stockholm. The inventory also makes it clear that the sets were frequently altered. It was possible, for instance, to expand a scene by a pair or two of side-wings to make it better suited to the deeper stage of Drottningholm. Further, the inventory is of great interest since it tells us about sets that no longer exist. It allows us to reconstruct the appearance of an entire stage decor though no more than a few pieces of it are still extant.

There are several instances of sets complete but for the backdrop. Here, inventory information, though perhaps only sketchy, can help us to arrive at a proper interpretation of what the entire set looked like. Let me give an example. The inventory record of a missing element for a garden set might run like this: "A drop representing three pavilions. In the center, Neptune with trident." Although this may seem the roughest of descriptions, it has enabled us to identify a scene drawn by Giuseppe Galli Bibiena in Vienna in 1740 as a study for a Drottningholm decor. Bibiena's setting is known to us from a contemporary engraving by J.A. Pfeffel.

There is one particular difficulty in cataloguing stage settings, and that is the bulk of the objects and consequently the awkwardness of handling them. Drottningholm's biggest sets are six meters high and the drops frequently measure six meters by eight. In order to make detailed inventory and adequate photographic documentation of such large objects, suitably large storage facilities are a necessity. The Theatre Museum has excellent facilities of this kind in the form of a clapboard-covered concrete repository which was specially built for the purpose in 1975. The really vital thing about the repository is that it has an automatic humidity-control system. The building looks something like a barn from the outside, and though it is rather big we think it fits in well with the other country buildings situated in the Drottningholm area. The size of the repository was dictated by the existing collection of sets from the Drottningholm and Rosersberg theatres. There is no real room for expansion.

The material from Drottningholm comprises 30 stage sets (most incomplete) which consist of 183 side-wings and 20 drops. The nine sets from Rosersberg consist of 92 side-wings and five drops. In addition, there are 205 set-pieces of varying kinds and sizes.

The side-wings are stored beside one another down the long sides of the building. Each is held in a special wooden frame which runs in a rail arrangement in the ceiling. This makes it easy to pull a side-wing to the central gangway for closer scrutiny. Side-wings belonging to the same scenery are stored together in the order they originally had for performance.

The drops are more difficult to handle. They are stored rolled up, hanging from the ceiling at both short ends of the building. With the help of laths and a cranking mechanism, two people can lower them.

The larger set-pieces are kept behind the drops at one short side of the building and the smaller ones on shelves at the opposite end. They are grouped together according to what they are or represent: camps, cabinets, doors, masks, statues, bushes, trees, and so on.

The cataloguing work is pursued according to established museum practice. First we have photography. This includes coverage of every object in black and white as well as color. The black-and-white work (front and back views) is done on 6-by-6-centimeter Ilford film. The color work on the side-wings with 35-millimeter Kodachrome, and on the drops with larger size Ektachrome. All color work is double, that is with two cameras providing two originals. One set is mounted and used in day-to-day work. The other is archived unmounted and is only intended for use in an emergency. The work has been done in daylight conditions and with a flash.

The descriptive work takes place during and after photographing the objects. We maintain data about materials and mode of construction, painting technique and color, original notations made on the objects themselves, together with measurements and present condition. In the second phase of the cataloguing procedure, we make extensive objects. The catalogue description consists of the following elements:

1. *Main category* (for example, side-wing, set-piece)
2. *Representation* (e.g., the object represents or reproduces a statue or an urn.
3. *Material, color, and painting technique*
4. *How made*
5. *Inscriptions* (all cited)
6. *Measurements* (height and breadth in centimeters)
7. *Condition* (first the overall condition such as: good fairly good, bad or very bad; followed by types of damage described in the same manner)
8. *Other information and comments*
9. *References* (archive sources and bibliography).

An actual object might appear in the catalogue in this way:

1. Set-piece
2. Skeleton with scythe and shroud
3. Distemper on cardboard; yellow, black, and white

4. Pieces of cardboard glued together, nailed to laths with an angular support on a footplate. Holes for stage screws
5. XLII
6. h 102, b 60. Footplate 30 x 60
7. Good general condition. Minor patches of damage from moisture and wear, rust around the nail-heads, breaks in the laths. Modern repair with veneer, masonite, and bank-iron
8. Left part of the footplate visible, indicating that a piece of cardboard is missing. Handle of the scythe probably cut off.
9. The 1806 Inventory: XLII "A figure representing Death, with cardboard scythe." Beijer op. cit., page 87

The exact description of an entire stage scene, comprising various connected parts, runs as follows: Please refer to illustrative plates.

First we have "DTM 206/1975 A - Q", which is our inventory number. After this comes the text:

Stage decor

representing a pillared hall in the Ionic style, consisting of seven pairs of side-wings, four framed backdrops, and two practicable staircases. Side-wings and backdrops are painted with distemper on cloth, stretched on lath frames. The buildings are picked out on the drops and side-wings in pale rose-gray; festoons and decorative ornaments are in green and various flower colors

A.

Left-hand side-wings closest to the proscenium opening. Inscription: "Number 1 in the 3rd 4674 M", wooden block with an iron loop to which a rope is attached.

Wear in places where the cloth rests against the transverse laths. The cloth patched in two places.

Measurements: h 563, b 166 centimeters.

[The letters B - Q follow in order, each side-wing being described in the same manner as in A.]

M = designation in the 1808 Inventory:

"An Ionic temple with garlands of flowers around the columns, 14 side-wings, tall or 7 levels."

M Backdrop:

"Backdrop for the Ionic temple at Malmen [i.e. the location], consisting of 4 frames representing architectural forms of modern Ionic composition."

M Borders:

"An Ionic temple; 6 borders, namely 1, 2, 3, 4, and 6, painted with buildings and festoons, apparently for the Ionic temple. The old inscription reads 'Wibiena' [i.e. Bibiena], located in a recess to the right under the ceiling."

The final entry reads:
References: Agne Beijer, *Slottsteatrarna pa Drottningholm och Gripsholm.* Malmo 1937, picture caption Plate *XX,* page *00;* Per Bjurstrom, *Teaterdekoration i Sverige.* Stockholm 1964, page *00.*

A close study of the various components of this stage décor reveals that it has been increased by two pairs of side-wings. This is evident from the re-marking which has obviously been done on the side-wings. Closer scrutiny of the technique used to paint the extra pairs of side-wings also shows quite clearly that a somewhat different technique has been used or the work has been done by a different artist.

The Types of Damage Encountered

The first thing to be noted is that the sets belonging to the theatre at Gripsholm are generally in better condition than those of Drottningholm. The Gripsholm sets are stored in the castle attics, not far from the auditorium of the theatre. They have rested there for a very considerable time and as far as we can tell they have not been moved for the past 150 years. The rooms are unheated but they are dry and ventilated, so it is rare for the sets to show any damage from damp or water. The Gripsholm borders and drops, on the other hand, have been stored hanging from the flies and do show some damage of this kind.

The Drottningholm sets were kept for about 120 years on stage. The drops were hung from the flies and side-wings and set-pieces were stood close together along the sides of the stage. Since the 1920s, the pieces have been moved on occasion to other storage sites of varying suitability. They have been standing too close together in their new locations. Leaky roofs have often let to water damage.

It is sometimes quite difficult to tell the difference between old and new damage. The most common form of damage is that of wear and tear, caused by the tight string of the pieces with consequent pressing of the laths against the painted cloth. Often fairly frequent forms of damage are caused by water or damp. Much of this type of damage probably occurred in our own time, and much of clumsy mending from the 1940s and 1950s has obliterated old inscriptions and markings. Other types of common damage are cracked or split laths and crushed or broken edges of profiles. As to the set-peices of cardboard, damage and repair is very frequent. Occasionally, we come across the effects of mold, but only on cardboard and wood. It seems that the distemper has not undergone any change at all, aside from the particles which have been lost from the surface. Its luster and life appear to be as real today as they were more than 200 years ago.

What kinds of repair can we tolerate, then? The only answer is that which aims at halting ongoing deterioration of some kind, and to take as few steps as possible. The important thing is, of course, to maintain the materials of the original pieces in as intact a state as we can. In addition to simple repair work such as the refurbishing of profiles, much labor has been expended on repairing the drops. Tears and holes in the material have been mended or patched with new cloth of equivalent quality, and new laths have been attached. This was necessary to avoid even greater damage: every time the drops were hung up, tears tended to grow, and broken laths injured the material by stretching it wrongly.

Some objects are in very poor condition, particularly the set-pieces made of sheets of cardboard glued together. They are sometimes in such bad condition that they seem impossible to identify. This "flotsam" is not worked on as much as other objects, yet it is important that the items are catalogued and stored properly. Nobody can tell what information they may yield at some future date: one such scrap might turn out to be the missing part of some larger structure.

The cataloguing work at Drottningholm–done in the way I have tried to describe–will soon be finished, at least as far as the descriptions and photographs are concerned. With its easily accessible information, the catalogue will now serve as a starting-point for further systematic comparisons. These studies will, we hope, result in a tenable hypothetical chronology. The catalogue will also enhance our ability to reconstruct the entire scope of use of the décor and will better enable us to map the activities and work methods of the various set painters.

Our institute plans to publish an English translation of the catalogue: a discursive part followed by a section containing the photographic documentation. The unique collection of scenic decor at Drottningholm and Gripsholm has its roots in a cultural tradition common to all of Europe. Our goal will have been achieved when full information about our collection can be spread outside the narrow borders of my country.

SOME ORIGINAL EARLY 19th CENTURY STAGE DECORATIONS IN THE LUDWIGSBURG COURT THEATRE: PROBLEMS OF CONSERVATION AND PRESENTATION

by Harald Zielske

Ludwigsburg Castle (about ten miles north of Stuttgart, the capital of the West German federal state of Baden-Württemberg) is one of the largest and most elaborate German baroque castles. Fortunately, it was not at all affected by the widespread destruction of architectural monuments of this kind during the second world war. It was erected from 1704 onward by Eberhard Ludwig, Duke of Württemberg, who employed several architects, mostly Italians, for this gigantic project; the castle was not yet fully completed in its interior when the Duke died in 1733. The Court Theatre, of which up to that year only the building itself was constructed, is an almost separate part of the vast complex of buildings of which the castle is composed. The auditorium and stage of the theatre came into existence in 1758 during the reign of Duke Carl Eugen. The theatre was inaugurated in the month of May of that year, and was then used frequently by Carl Eugen until 1775.

A second period of regular use of the theatre came not before 1802, and lasted until 1817, under Duke Friedrich II (after 1806, King Friedrich I of Württemberg.) In 1805, Napoleon, on his way to fight Franz II of Austria, saw a performance of Mozart's *Don Giovanni* in this theatre. After the death of King Friedrich in 1817, Ludwigsburg Castle was no longer the official residence of the kings of Württemberg, and consequently the Court Theatre fell almost completely out of use. Only some touring companies played there in the 1820s and in the 1840s, but after that the edifice seems to have been practically forgotten as a theatre. It was temporarily used for the Württemberg State Archives, and only after the last war - to be precise: from 1954 onward - it was at first restored and the stage adapted for the exigencies of modern performing practice, and then came into regular use again as a theatre: this, however, only for a couple of performances a year.

HARALD ZIELSKE serves with the Institute fur Theaterwissenschaft of the Free University of Berlin.

It is certainly due to this very long "sleeping beauty" existence, lasting from the early nineteenth to the second half of the twentieth century, that the Ludwigsburg Court Theatre offers itself as a unique monument and relic of German theatre history of the age of Goethe and Schiller, of the so-called German *Klassic*. In the store-room behind the stage there are a large number of original stage decorations dating from that time of the more frequent use of the theatre in the years between 1802 and 1817.

In 1964 and 1965, a team of students from the *Institut für Theaterwissenschaft* at the Freie Universität Berlin, under my supervision, visited Ludwigsburg Castle and its Court Theatre several times. We inspected all the existent parts of stage decorations very thoroughly, counted and registered them, and made hundreds of photographs. In all we counted 13 back drops, plus one front-curtain, two cut cloths, more than one hundred wings and a few set pieces. Most of the back drops show indoor scenes: halls in classicist or gothic style, a prison, two rural interior settings. Three of the back drops are of open-air scenery: a wooden landscape or a garden. Of the existent wings, a certain number clearly belong to one or the other of the 13 back drops. So it was possible for our "archeological team" to reconstruct several complete scenery settings on the stage of the Court Theatre. By this manoeuver, we succeeded in forming sort of stylistic totality out of the appearance of the auditorium on the one hand, and the appearance of the stage on the other.

As far as I know, the Ludwigsburg stock of original stage decorations of the age of German classicism is absolutely singular and completely unique. Nowhere else have so many original elements of theatre productions of the past been discovered. What we knew about the appearance of a stage at the time when Goethe was director of the Weimar Court Theatre and Schiller wrote his dramas to be performed there, or when August Wilhelm Iffland served concurrently as director, playwright and star-actor at the *Königliches National-Theater* in Berlin, was brought before our eyes by the pictorial media of sketches, designs or copperprints.

I cannot determine for certain the authorship of all these original decoration sets in Ludwigsburg. They seem to have been painted. Except for one landscape back drop, which for certain reasons may be of an earlier date, approximately at the same period; a time when the Ludwigsburg Court Theatre was in regular use and consequently in need of a larger and stylistically up-to-date stock of stage decorations. As the decorations obviously are of classicist style, they could only have been manufactured between 1802 and 1817, the second period in which the theatre regularly saw a greater number of annual stage productions. It is most likely that the decorations were designed, or at least initiated and stylistically supervised, by Nikolaus Friedrich von Thouret, the classicist court architect of King Friedrich I of Württemberg. We know that Thouret was also in charge of the stage decoration of the Stuttgart and Ludwigsburg Court Theatres, just as the rebuilding of the auditorium in the Ludwigsburg theatre is his work. Unfortunately, we do not have any authentic sketches or designs for stage decorations in the hand of Thouret, so that we cannot be absolutely sure that the existent stage decorations in Ludwigsburg are his.

The artistic value of the Ludwigsburg stage decorations may be called moderate. They are certainly not of the same high quality as those designed by Karl Friedrich Schinkel for Mozart's *The Magic Flute,* or several Spontini operas produced at the Berlin ***Königliche Schauspiele,*** the Court Theatre of the King of Prussia. Schinkel's decorations are undoubtedly the high-lights of German classicist stage scenery, which the Ludwigsburg decorations cannot match. However, they may very well be compared with those stage decorations invented by the stage designer and scene-painter Friedrich Christian Beuther (1777-1856), who for some years was employed by Goethe for the Weimar Court Theatre. With Beuther's sceneries, many of which have been preserved in original sketches, designs, and prints, those from Ludwigsburg are obviously on the same artistic level, as a comparison of some examples can easily prove. So, by rediscovering the original Ludwigsburg stage decorations of the early nineteenth century, we are now able to procure a definite and authentic impression of what the stage looked like during a theatre performance in the age of classicism, the age of Goethe and Schiller, and in the Weimar Court Theatre itself. The then so-frequently produced plays by Kotzebue and Iffland, and the great dramas of Schiller all used the kind of scenery extant at the Ludwigsburg Court Theatre, and it is amazing to think that, via these decorations, we have a real part of those transitory, long-gone performances still at our hand—so to speak, "live" before our eyes.

However, the Ludwigsburg stage decorations do not only bring back part of a historical past. They also confront us with a severe problem: the problem of conserving and adequately presenting their documentary value. The greater part of the decorations, back drops as well as wings, are today in a very deplorable state of preservation. During the long decades of disuse, they were neglected when being stored and moved around from one place to another within the theatres building, handled without care, proper understanding and respect for their historical value. Consequently, they suffered heavy damage, and, tragically. I have proof that even in recent years some of the existent back drops for some reason unknown to me deliberately were destroyed. For in the administration office of the castle, I have seen several photos of back drops taken in the 1930s and 1940s but when we rediscovered the whole complex of decorations in the 1960s no trace of these back drops was left.

The same has to be said for the wings and the set pieces. Bulky and no longer in use. they seem to have been considered as some kind of waste, and consequently many of them must have been destroyed and simply thrown away. Among the still existent 115 wings and set pieces, we found only very few complete sets of side wings fitting to the likewise existent back drops. For further back drops, there remained a non-sufficient number of pairs of wings, or only the wings of one lateral part of the whole scenery. So only two complete sceneries - a *sala del grotto* and a classic hall - could be reconstructed on the stage.

What conclusion has to be drawn out of this rather depressing result of an important theatre historical discovery? Apart from this special case of the Ludwigsburg decorations, the conclusion must be general. It cannot be doubted that in many older and ill-used theatre, not only in Germany but in other countries as well, there still do exist such objects of utmost historical value as the Ludwigsburg classicist stage decorations. Objects that can tell their historical message, if I may say so, much more directly and impressively than do those documents with which we are normally occupied in our archives and collections: I mean, the easier-to-handle scenery sketches and designs, scene prints and photos.

Therefore, I think, there should be a firm commitment from all theatre archivists, theatre museum directors and their assistants, and from each and every theatre-historian in general. Wherever such important theatre historical monuments as original stage decorations are known to be existent or are rediscovered, they must urge the authorities-in-charge to do their utmost for the conservation and proper presentation of these so valuable monuments. We all know that some European countries already have given admirable examples of how to handle this matter, and I simply need to recall some of them, the places and the theatres: Sweden with its Drottningholm Court Theatre (original stage decorations of the late eighteenth century), Czechoslovakia with the small Court Theatres in Krumlov and Leitomischl (early nineteenth century), German Democratic Republic with the collection of back drops in the famous Hoftheater of the Duke of Meiningen in Meiningen (late nineteenth century).

The case of the Ludwigsburg decorations reminds us, however, that the examples just quoted should not remain the only ones in this field of a theatre-historical archeology. I think that in every country, in which theatre history is not considered as a mere hobby, an obsolete and a somewhat exotic occupation of a few romantic minded spirits, but where it is valued as a genuine historical research discipline, we should try to stimulate a systematic search for still existing older stage decorations. And where we know of such objects or learn about their rediscovery, we should strive with all our force for the conservation and the adequate presentation of such invaluable theatre-historical monuments.

There has much been done in many countries for the conservation and even reconstruction of historical theatre buildings and especially auditoriums. I cite just a few memorable examples from my own country, the Federal Republic of Germany: the *Markgräfliches Opernhaus* in Bayreuth, the *Markgrafentheater* in Erlangen, the *Cuvillies-* or *Altes Residenz-Theater* in Munich, the *Schlosstheater* in Schwetzingen; or, the entire reconstruction of a nineteenth-century theatre, a reconstruction practically out of nothing after the radical destruction of the theatre by bombs during the last war: the Munich opera house, the so called *National-Theater*.

Considering these examples, the money, and the efforts that have gone into them, I think that is is not sufficient to show care and interest only for historical auditoriums in old theatre buildings. For a serious theatre historian, it must be absolutely obligatory to care also for the indispensable correlate of a historical auditorium, which is the appearance of a carefully reconstructed historical stage. We all know that it is impossible to reconstruct the historical theatre performance as a whole—the work of the actor, the work of the stage producer are gone for ever. But as the Ludwigsburg stage decorations teach us unmistakably, we can at least retain a very important part of that lost totality of a historical theatre performance by reconstructing or even simply preserving the historical stage in its original shape and appearance. We all should learn this lesson, which the Ludwigsburg case teaches us, and we should learn it as quickly as possible, before it is to late and the destruction of theatre-historical monuments continues.